Submarines

Submarines

ANTONY PRESTON

GALLERY BOOKS
An imprint of W.H. Smith Publishers Inc.
112 Madison Avenue
New York, New York 10016

A Bison Book

Published by Gallery Books
A Division if W H Smith Publishers Inc.
112 Madison Avenue
New York, New York 10016

Produced by
Bison Books Corp.
17 Sherwood Place,
Greenwich, CT 06830
USA

Printed in Hong Kong

1 2 3 4 5 6 7 8 9 10

ISBN 0-8317-7978-0

CONTENTS

THE FIRST U-BOATS

For centuries designers dreamed of submarines but the first practical design did not appear until 1578 when an Englishman, William Bourne described a submersible boat. He mastered a concept which eluded many later submarine designers by providing a simple mechanical means of varying the boat's total weight. He also solved the lack of fresh air by providing a hollow mast, but there is no record in his description of any form of propulsion, nor of any purpose, peaceful or otherwise, for his boat. The Dutch physician, van Drebbel, went a step further, and in 1624 built two submersibles propelled by oars. The purpose of submarines up to the middle of the eighteenth century was largely restricted to salvage or construction work on the sea bed, in other words an extension of the diving bell's capability.

An American, Robert Fulton, took the submarine a step further with his *Nautilus* in 1799 but despite convincing demonstrations neither the French or the British wanted anything to do with him. With nothing but hand-propulsion available and only the crudest of close-range weapons it was still nothing more than a toy.

In 1850 a Bavarian artillery sergeant called Wilhelm Bauer produced a submarine called the *Brandtaucher* or 'Fire Diver.' The first voyage in December 1850 was successful but little more than a month later the *Brandtaucher* was lost in Kiel harbor. Bauer was not discouraged by this setback, however, and produced a number of other designs for underwater craft. In 1855 he was allowed to build an improved 52 feet submarine called the *Seeteufel* or 'Sea Devil' for the Imperial Russian Navy.

The 'Davids,' built during the American Civil War by the Confederate States to break the Federal blockade, marked the next step forward. The original 'David' was hardly a submarine rather a submersible torpedo boat but she was driven by a steam engine. The 'Davids' did score some successes but their cost was exorbitant; two warships sunk and a third damaged for the loss of two submersibles (which had each sunk once before during training, with the loss of their entire crews).

In 1878 a Liverpool clergyman, the Reverend George Garrett, built a small egg-shaped boat and a year later started a second boat, christened the *Resurgam*. It was 40 feet long and used steam on the surface. Before submerging a full head of steam was raised to provide latent heat in special storage tanks. The Swedish arms manufacturer Thorsten Nordenfelt put up fresh capital to allow the building of a new boat at Stockholm to a design by Garrett. This boat was sold to Greece in 1883 and Turkey ordered two more in 1886 but they were not a success. They were, however, the first to use the Whitehead automobile torpedo. For the first time a submarine could attack a target from a safe distance.

The submarine still needed a workable means of underwater propulsion. The answer lay in the electric motor but early electricity generators were too heavy. The accumulator battery was also very heavy, but it did offer a way around the problem. A young Spanish naval officer designed a boat in 1886, powered by two 30hp electric motors using current stored in accumulators. The French soon grasped the implications and started work on designs of their own. In April 1887 the first submarine, the *Gymnote* or 'Eel,' was laid down. Her armament was a single 14-inch torpedo tube in the bow, and her electric batteries drove her at a theoretical maximum speed of 6½ knots. However the *Gymnote* relied totally on her accumulator batteries and these had to be recharged by a generator ashore or in another ship.

The next submarine ordered, the *Gustav Zédé*, was much larger. Although she gave a lot of trouble she provided invaluable experience, and convinced the French that the submarine was worth developing. In February 1896 the Minister of Marine proposed an open competition to produce designs for a 200-ton submarine with a range of 100 miles on the surface, and no

Below: The CSS *C L Hunley*, a hand-cranked submersible, sank the Federal sloop *Housatonic* during the American Civil War.

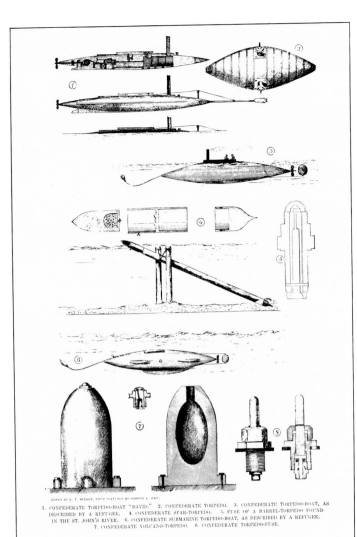

1. CONFEDERATE TORPEDO-BOAT "DAVID." 2. CONFEDERATE TORPEDO. 3. CONFEDERATE TORPEDO-BOAT, AS DESCRIBED BY A REFUGEE. 4. CONFEDERATE SPAR-TORPEDO. 5. FUSE OF A BARREL-TORPEDO FOUND IN THE ST. JOHN'S RIVER. 6. CONFEDERATE SUBMARINE TORPEDO-BOAT, AS DESCRIBED BY A REFUGEE. 7. CONFEDERATE VOLCANO-TORPEDO. 8. CONFEDERATE TORPEDO-FUSE.

Above: A modern model of Bushnell's *Turtle* incorporates the results of the latest historical research.
Left: Confederate 'torpedoes' and torpedo boats included not only submersibles but mines as well.
Below: The French *Amphitrite* (1906) served for twenty years.

Top: The Italian FIAT firm built the 'F' Class to the designs of General Laurent.
Above: The *Naiade* of 1901 was too small to be effective and was out of service by 1914.
Below: French submarines like the *Clorinde* (1907) were noted for their low silhouette.

fewer than 29 designs were submitted from all over the world. The winner was a Frenchman, Maxime Laubeuf, whose remarkable boat, the *Narval* had two propulsion systems, a 220hp steam engine for surface running and an 80hp electric motor for running underwater. But most important of all, the steam engine could also run a dynamo to recharge the batteries, and so the effective range of the *Narval* was much greater than the all-electric boats.

Despite the importance of Laubeuf his fame has been eclipsed by that of John P Holland, who had been designing submarines since 1875. In 1893 he entered a United States' Navy competition to choose a submarine design. Only two other inventors submitted designs, Lake and Baker. The Baker boat quickly dropped out of the competition and as Simon Lake did not complete his prototype promptly the Ordnance Bureau awarded the contract to Holland. The boat, called the *Plunger*, was launched in 1897 after a number of changes and delays. So many changes were made against the designer's wishes that he withdrew from the contract and ordered his Holland Boat Company to build a second submarine at his own expense. His faith was justified by the total failure of the *Plunger* to pass her trials; the boat was never accepted by the Navy and the contract was cancelled. The trials of the *Holland*, by comparison, were a great success, and the US Navy bought her in 1900. By a year later a further seven of similar type were building and the British had taken out a license to build five for the Royal Navy.

The *Holland* design differed from the French *Narval* in several ways. She also had a dual propulsion system, but used a 45hp gasoline engine for surface running, giving more power for less weight as well as more reliable starting and stopping. This produced two advantages, the boat could be smaller and it could dive faster than the French boat.

The Germans, of all the major naval powers, were the last to show an interest, for Admiral Tirpitz saw submarines as a threat to his plans for a big battle-fleet. However the firm of Krupps built a small submarine for Russia in 1902–03, and were then asked by the Russians to tender for three more boats. These were known as the *Karp* class, and a fourth unit, almost identical, became the German *U.1* in 1906. She had a Körting kerosene engine, which was better than the gasoline engine of the Hollands. It had one severe drawback, however. It gave off dense clouds of smoke which gave away the submarine's position, and only when the Diesel engine was perfected was surface propulsion satisfactory.

By 1904, therefore, the broad outlines of the modern submarine were settled. The three big advances, the electric accumulator battery, the diesel engine and the self-propelled tor-

pedo were to be steadily improved as the years went by, but no other fundamental change was necessary for another 50 years. The submarines of 1904 were essentially the types that would revolutionize naval warfare in 1914, yet ten years earlier only two workable submarines existed. It had been a remarkably short period of gestation.

Although much lip-service had been paid to the effect of submarines on naval warfare the world's navies in 1914 had little idea of how to use them. All the belligerents and the neutrals regarded themselves as bound by the provisions of International Law and the Hague Convention of 1899 concerning the conduct of war at sea. It was assumed that a sub-

Above: The German 'UB' Class of small U-Boats proved to be useful in the North Sea. *UB.4* is pictured at Zeebrugge, an important German submarine base in World War I.

marine, like any other warship, was not permitted to fire on an unarmed merchant ship not acting in a hostile manner. The submarine would have to stop the merchant ship and examine her papers to ascertain that she was in fact trading on behalf of the enemy. If the papers indicated that she was carrying contraband the ship would have a prize crew put aboard to sail her to a port of examination. The submarine could, of course, sink the ship and forego the prize money, and if the weather was too

rough for taking to the boats the crew were to be taken aboard the submarine as prisoners.

The Prize Regulations, as they were called, favored the British and the French with their large merchant fleets, but they took little account of the peculiar nature of the submarine. To stop and search a merchant ship the submarine had to come to the surface, thereby forfeiting her principal advantage. Her tiny crew was too small to allow a prize crew to be spared and there was no room aboard for prisoners.

A submarine which endeavored to keep to these rules would either expose herself to counter-attacks from enemy warships or would be able to sink no more than one or two ships on each cruise. In spite of these drawbacks, however, some thought had been given to using submarines against commerce, and on 20 October 1914 *U.17* made history by capturing the small steamer *Glitra* off Norway.

Most naval officers still regarded the enemy's warships as the true target for the submarine, and the first successes bore out this belief. As soon as war broke out both the British and Germans sent out submarines to observe and report on warship movements. The British set up a patrol line in the Heligoland Bight, and acting on reports from these submarines planned a successful raid on the German light forces late in August 1914. Similarly the Germans sent their U-Boats out on an offensive patrol as far north as the Orkneys, to find out what the British were doing.

Both sides were disappointed. The British found that their torpedoes were running under their targets because the warhead was heavier than the pre-war practice head, while the Germans found that extended cruising put an unexpected strain on machinery. The limited field of vision through a periscope

made target identification much harder than anyone had imagined in peacetime, and there were many wrong guesses. The early successes against warships were as much the result of the victim's carelessness as the skill of submariners.

On 22 September a single U-Boat, *U.9*, sank three armored cruisers, the *Aboukir, Cressy* and *Hogue*. These three old ships, with little protection against modern torpedoes and carrying large crews of reservists, were known to be vulnerable and the order cancelling their patrols was already drafted. The senior officer of the squadron assumed that the first ship had been mined, and so Kapitänleutnant Otto Weddigen was given time to reload his torpedo tubes and work *U.9* into an ideal attacking position between the two remaining cruisers, with both forward and after tubes bearing. Weddigen's reputation as the first U-Boat 'ace' was confirmed when three weeks later he torpedoed another old cruiser, the *Hawke* off Aberdeen. Yet here again, the British cruiser was lying stopped in the open sea to transfer mail, and there were other examples of ships piping 'Hands to Bathe' or steaming slowly in waters known to be patrolled by U-Boats.

The Royal Navy had moved its main fleet base from the southern dockyards to a new base at Rosyth before the war, but on the outbreak of war the Grand Fleet moved to Scapa Flow, a large natural anchorage in the Orkneys. The news of the U-Boats' foray to the Orkneys was followed by a submarine scare in the Flow itself, and although no U-Boat got into Scapa Flow throughout the war the fear was enough to paralyze the Grand Fleet. Until Scapa Flow could be defended with nets, blockships, guns and searchlights it was necessary to send the whole fleet away to the west coast of Scotland. This was the first major strategic victory scored by submarines, for they had forced an entire fleet away from its chosen area of operations, and had the Germans been in a position to take advantage of it they might have caught the Royal Navy badly off balance. As things turned out there were not enough U-Boats and those that

Below: *E.6* was one of the famous 'E' Class, which formed the backbone of the Royal Navy's submarine force in World War I.

existed were not yet reliable enough to be risked far from their bases, while the High Seas Fleet did little to take advantage of the British withdrawal. The chance passed, and once the Grand Fleet returned to the Orkneys it refastened its grip on the German Fleet; its base remained inviolate right to the end.

When war broke out the German Navy had 29 U-Boats (U-Boat = *Unterseeboot*) in service. The original boat, *U.1* had been developed into the *U.27* Class, of which *U.30* was still to complete, but a further 20 boats were on order. This modest program reflects the German High Command's obsession with the surface fleet, and for a long time the admirals continued to think that the main role of their U-Boats was to wage a war of attrition against British warships, either by direct attack or by using the surface fleet to draw the British fleet into a 'submarine trap.'

The German Navy's submarines proved to be well-designed and the current class was put into quantity production. A new small or coastal type, the 'UB' Class was also started to make use of available Körting kerosene engines, and the first mine-layers or 'UC' Class were also ordered. In the summer of 1915 the British were mystified by reports of damage to merchant ships, but in July 1915 a steamer reported that she had collided with a submerged object, and when divers went down they found that the newly completed *UC.2* had blown herself up with her own mines.

The sinking of the *Glitra* by *U.17* encouraged the German naval staff in the growing belief that submarines could and should be used against British shipping. The ruthlessness with which Great Britain enforced the blockade also weakened any scruples entertained about violation of international law. For example the British even declared foodstuffs to be contraband, claiming that the German government had commandeered all food supplies. Allied propaganda made good use of any mistakes made by the U-Boats; for example the sinking of the SS *Amiral Ganteaume* by *U.24* off Cap Gris Nez in October 1914 was de-

Above: Early U-Boats are moored at Hamburg, including (from left) *U.22, U.20, U.19* and *U.21.*

nounced as an atrocity because she was carrying Belgian refugees, but knowing how little the U-Boat's commander could have seen through his periscope it is more likely that he mistook her for a French troopship. The time for a torpedo shot was often limited to a few seconds, during which the submarine CO was supposed to count numbers of people on board, boats, guns and even where they were positioned; guns mounted forward were classed as offensive armament whereas guns mounted aft were defensive.

Even without any flouting of the Germans' self-imposed

Below: The German U-Boat *U.35* sinks the British merchantman SS *Parkgate* by gunfire.

restrictions, the losses were heavy, 32,000 tons of British and 15,900 tons of French and neutral shipping sunk in January 1915 alone. By March the total had risen to 80,700 tons for that month, and two months later to 185,000 tons. Neutral opinion was outraged, and the United States was particularly angry, because the needs of the British and French war economies had opened new markets to all countries exporting war material of any kind. There was a residue of anti-British feeling in the United States, and the blockade did prevent some American exporters from sending goods to Germany, but the vast increase in British and French demands more than replaced the lost German markets. In addition there was a sentimental attachment between France and the USA which went back to the days of Marquis de Lafayette, Admiral de Grasse and the War of Independence. American public opinion was violently inflamed against Germany by stories of the rape of Belgium, and the deaths of American citizens in torpedoed ships did nothing to help.

On 4 February 1915, Germany announced that a War Zone existed around the British Isles, in which British and French ships would be sunk without warning. The declaration added that it would not always be possible to avoid attacks on neutral shipping; in other words the U-Boats could now sink merchantmen 'at sight' unless they saw a neutral flag. If the neutral countries could have been persuaded to forbid their ships to trade with the Allies the German gamble might have paid off, but the British blockade meant that a refusal to trade with the Allies would mean virtual bankruptcy for most shipping companies as there was not enough trade with other countries to keep everyone in business.

A great help to the U-Boat offensive was the German Army's conquest of bases on the Belgian coast. After the initial German land advance was held at the Battle of the Marne the front stabilized with its flank resting on the Flanders coast at Nieuport. The German Navy set up a completely new naval base at Ostend, with light forces based there and at Zeebrugge. U-Boats were based at the inland port of Bruges and reached the open sea by canals to Zeebrugge and Ostend. These Flanders bases reduced the distance and increased the time the U-Boats could spend on patrol in the Western Approaches and the Bristol and St George's Channels, their best hunting-grounds. British minefields and net-barriers in the Dover Straits were not effective as the U-Boats soon learned to make the passage on the surface at night, when the chances of being spotted were slim. To encourage the British in their belief that the Dover Straits were blocked U-Boats from German ports making the 'northabout' passage around the Orkneys were even ordered to show themselves occasionally to the patrols. Part of the problem was the lack of an efficient British mine, as later experience was to

Above: The end of the road: *UC.91* and a sister boat are tied up alongside one of the giant U-Cruisers after being surrendered in 1918. Below: A German submarine takes the lifeboat of a sunk enemy steamer in tow, April 1917.

show that minefields were an important weapon against submarines. Above all there was no adequate way of sinking a submarine even if she gave away her presence, the principal tactic for a surface ship being to ram or try to hit the U-Boat with gunfire. Both these methods pre-supposed that the submarine was either submerging or running at periscope depth; once a submarine dived deeper she was not only immune but undetectable.

The Allies' answer to the U-Boat offensive of 1915 was to increase the number of patrols by impressing all manner of ships into service. The battle fleet was screened by destroyers, whose speed and maneuverability gave them some chance of racing to the spot where a submarine had dived. They could then ram or try to hit the conning tower with a lucky shot from their guns. After the initial losses no major warships moved anywhere without her destroyer escorts, and as a result no battleship of the Grand Fleet was torpedoed by a U-Boat at sea throughout the war, but there were not enough destroyers to spare for

Above left: A wartime scene shows UB III U-Boats tied up alongside a temder.
Left: Two U-Boats keep a mid-ocean rendezvous.

Above: *U.35* loads torpedoes before leaving for a wartime cruise in April 1917.
Above right: A U-Boat runs on the surface.

escorting merchant ships. The Auxiliary Patrol was formed out of the large number of steam yachts, trawlers and drifters available, and after being armed with guns they were sent off to hunt for submarines. But the Atlantic and the North Sea are large areas, and no matter how many patrols were maintained there was always space in which submarines could hide. The huge volume of shipping in and out of British ports meant that the U-Boats merely had to wait for their victims to come to them – if a patrol vessel appeared the submarine could submerge and wait until it was safe to come up again and begin the process of destruction again.

Nothing more clearly illustrates how easy it was than the tragedy of the *Lusitania*. Most British transatlantic liners had been taken over by the Royal Navy in August 1914 for conversion to armed merchant cruisers or troopships, but the *Lusitania* was kept in commercial service between Liverpool and New York.

Much has been made of the fact that the *Lusitania* was carrying explosives, according to her manifest 5500 cases of small-arms ammunition and fuse nose-caps, totalling 37 tons. It has even been claimed that she was armed, despite the absence of any evidence. The *Lusitania*'s small cargo (as a passenger liner she had in any case very little cargo-capacity, despite her size) comprised the most inert form of munitions in existence, and short of the ship catching fire there was little likelihood of it exploding.

When in due course on 7 May 1915 the *Lusitania* was torpedoed by *U.20* off Southern Ireland both sides for their own reasons tried to claim that the sinking had been planned. To the British it was all part of a plot to sink innocent ships, while the Germans claimed that as they knew of the *Lusitania*'s cargo their submarine was quite entitled to sink her. What both sides chose to ignore was that Kapitänleutnant Schwieger's own report showed that *U.20* had stumbled on the liner by chance.

The U-Boat had patrolled unsuccessfully in the Irish Sea for some days, and Schwieger had moved southwards to find more targets. He had been ordered to look out for troopships arriving from Canada and so headed for the Old Head of Kinsale, a popular landfall for transatlantic shipping. Schwieger was not disappointed, and soon saw smoke on the horizon. He was puzzled by the target's four funnels belching smoke, and assumed that he had stumbled on a submarine's worst enemy, a whole flotilla of destroyers. But then the 'flotilla' altered course, and to his joy Schwieger saw the massive bulk and four funnels of a

Above left: A blazing schooner sinks after being hit by gunfire from a U-Boat in mid-Atlantic.
Above: The 'commercial' U-Boat *Deutschland*.

large ship in the graticules of his periscope. On the assumption that most large liners were serving either as armed merchant cruisers or troopships, and as she carried no Red Cross markings to indicate a hospital ship he ordered one torpedo to be fired. The report made no mention of seeing guns, and as we have already mentioned, a submariner could see so little through a periscope that he would not have been looking for them, but it did mention a second explosion. This has been claimed to be the cargo of munitions 'tearing the heart out' of the ship, but any ordnance expert can testify to the fact that a quantity of rifle bullets and nose-caps some distance away from an explosion are unlikely to cause a further detonation. Schwieger himself attributed the second bang to boilers, coal or munitions, without further comment. If he was correct in thinking that his torpedo hit level with the funnels the more plausible explanation is that seawater rushing into the boiler-rooms caused an implosion of the boilers. A big liner of that vintage, with her numerous boiler-rooms, was doomed once flooding started on a large scale and the *Lusitania* went down rapidly with heavy loss of life. *U.20* slipped away unseen.

Below: The *R.2* was a British forerunner of the fast submarines of the post-1945 era. These streamlined craft exceeded 14 knots underwater as early as 1918.

Among the many dead were 159 American citizens, and the US government reaction was stronger than it had been previously. A note from Washington to Berlin demanded that U-Boats should refrain from torpedoing passenger ships. The Germans did not handle the diplomatic crisis tactfully, and maintained that they had warned passengers of the dangers, thereby giving further credence to the 'conspiracy' theory. The British, who had believed that the Germans would never dare to sink the *Lusitania*, were not averse to making capital out of the incident. Carefully skating round the point about the cargo (the contents of the manifest were published after the First World War), they connived at the idea of a planned sinking, although if anyone thought about the security implications, they would have realised that German agents would have had to be in command of the ship herself to achieve such a perfect interception.

The outcry forced the German government to slow down its onslaught on shipping, but in 1916 losses climbed steadily once more, until the monthly total reached over half a million tons. The Allies responded with 'Q-Ships,' decoy vessels fitted with concealed guns. The Q-Ship loitered in a likely area with the intention of luring an U-Boat to the surface for an easy sinking with her deck gun. If all went well a 'panic party' abandoned ship, leaving gun-crews aboard who would open fire as soon as the U-Boat came within range. Although a few spectacular suc-

cesses were scored the Q-Ship idea was greatly over-rated, and tied up skilled seamen who were needed elsewhere, without sinking enough submarines to justify itself. A variation on the decoy theme was to use trawlers and submarines together to stop U-Boats from shelling the fishing fleet. Among the trawler fleet would be one trawler towing, instead of a trawl, a small submarine. The submarine was in touch with the trawler by means of a telephone link, and could cast off the towing wire. The idea actually worked twice, although each time technical snags nearly ruined everything, and the submarines each sank a U-Boat.

The Allies also armed merchant ships to enable them to fight off U-Boats. In practice the provision of a small gun on the poop of a tramp steamer did little but boost the crew's morale. However bad the shooting from a submarine's deck-gun the shooting from the average steamer was probably much worse.

The arming of merchant ships inevitably led the Germans into upgunning their submarines. The 'cruiser-submarine' with her medium-caliber guns had a tremendous moral effect, and in Britain there was even talk of having to arm merchantmen with 6-inch or 7.5-inch guns. What the advocates of big submarine guns ignored was that against the thin plating of a merchant ship a 4-inch shell is as good as a 6-inch, bearing in mind that a submarine had such poor fire-control that she would have to approach relatively close to allow her gun-crew to achieve hits.

The theory of the cruiser-submarine was that she could drive off small warships by out-ranging their guns, but in practice no submarine was likely to win such a contest. One hit or near miss from a shell could damage the submarine sufficiently to prevent her from diving, whereas the submarine's shooting would have to be exceptionally good to cripple even a small warship.

The first German cruiser-submarines were actually converted from a series of big mercantile submarines, built in 1915–16 to run cargoes through the blockade. Their purpose was two-fold: to bring in special materials needed for the armaments industry and to prove to neutral opinion that Germany was not being strangled by the blockade. Unlike other submarines the cargo-carrying submarines were named, and the first, *Deutschland*, left Kiel in June 1916 carrying a small cargo of mail, chemical dyes and precious stones for Baltimore. She presented a tricky legal problem for the US Customs authorities but as she was clearly not armed she was entitled to be treated as a commercial vessel. The effect on the Americans was tremendous; crowds flocked to see the submarine after her arrival on 9 July, and again when she sailed for Bremen three weeks later, loaded with copper, nickel, silver and zinc. Although the size of her cargo would never have made her a commercial proposition the *Deutschland*'s propaganda value to Germany was enormous, but an attempt to repeat the performance backfired.

A second cargo-submarine, the *Bremen*, set out, bound for Newport, Rhode Island. She was accompanied by *U.53* under Kapitänleutnant Hans Rose, who had orders to 'blow a path' for the *Bremen* through any British warships which tried to bar her passage. Unfortunately British mines were more effective in doing the job and the *Bremen* disappeared without trace somewhere off the Orkneys, with the result that *U.53* arrived at Newport on 7th October by herself. The US Navy suddenly found itself with a belligerent nation's submarine lying off one of its naval bases, a situation for which the rule book did not cater. While the Navy frantically badgered the State Department and everyone else for instructions, Hans Rose finished

the amusing chat that he had been having with the naval officers at Newport and left as quietly as he had arrived. But what followed undid any goodwill that *U.53*'s visit might have engendered, for the U-Boat started to sink shipping within sight of Nantucket lightship. Rose was convinced that his mysterious visit had left the US Navy and Government with a deep impression of how powerful Germany's submarines were; before he had left Germany he had been told by Commodore Hermann Bauer (the chief of the U-Boat Arm) that bold action would silence the anti-German party in America and would result in the restrictions on the U-Boats being lifted. The reasoning behind this forecast is hard to follow, and the Germans evidently understood very little of American attitudes. In fact the Americans became even more worried about German intentions, while the US Navy started to take the submarine threat seriously indeed. Germany's leaders, furthermore, did not feel that the time was right to launch a second unrestricted U-Boat campaign, and so the second attempt to break the British blockade was also a failure. The *Deutschland* was converted to a military submarine with two torpedo tubes and four guns. Six more were ordered in February 1917, and the class were numbered *U151–157*, the *Deutschland* becoming *U.155*.

Not until February 1917 was permission given for unrestricted U-Boat warfare. It was a gamble, for the High Command knew that it was only a matter of time before the Americans came into

Far left: Crewmen of a U-Boat are wrapped up to keep out the cold and the damp.
Left: U-Boats pictured at their base at Bruges. Many German submarines were based at captured Belgian ports.
Right: A U-Boat crew strikes down a torpedo.
Below: *U.8* sinks after being damaged by a British destroyer in March 1915.

the war to rescue the French and British. If they could force the British to sue for peace the attitude of the Americans was irrelevant. With German submarines in command of the North Atlantic the Americans could not intervene in Europe, and Germany would then be free to deal with France at her leisure. It was an appealing proposition and one that the Navy favored. The High Seas Fleet knew that after the Battle of the Skagerrak (Jutland) in May 1916 that it could never win, and that it had been extremely lucky to escape destruction. Thereafter its best officers, petty officers and seamen were drafted to U-Boats and torpedo-boats in increasing numbers. The U-Boats ordered since 1914 were also coming into service, and the daily average of boats at sea was rising steadily from no more than 10 in mid-1915 to 30 by the end of 1916. In mid-1917 the figure would exceed 40 U-Boats, with more to come, and the Germans knew that the time had come to act.

The first results justified all the claims made by the U-Boat Arm. Within weeks the shipping losses rocketed to nearly 800,000 tons (April 1917). The British countermeasures proved quite inadequate, and no matter how many warships, auxiliary patrol vessels and Q-Ships were deployed, one ship in every four that entered the War Zone was certain to be sunk. When the United States entered the war in the same month, Admiral Sims of the US Navy went to London to confer with Sir John Jellicoe, the First Sea Lord, and was appalled to hear that the naval war was being lost, and that food stocks in the British Isles would only last six weeks. Every weapon that could be used against the submarine had been tried, and the Admiralty no longer knew which way to turn.

Yet the oldest weapon of all had not been tried, the sailing of merchant shipping in groups under the protection of warships. Convoy had been in use from the fourteenth century until the end of the Napoleonic Wars but somehow the impact of more recent technology had blinded naval officers to the simple fact that an attack on merchant shipping was easiest to defend against if the merchant ships were concentrated in groups. It seems an obvious statement to make, but the sea is a big area, and individual merchantmen could never conceivably be allocated their own escort. Convoy was the only way in which a limited number of warships could hope to protect the Allies' vast merchant fleet.

The argument over convoy took time to resolve. The British Prime Minister was in favor after hearing the views of the Cabinet Secretary, Maurice Hankey, and naval officers in the Trade Division. The Admiralty Board fought hard against it, however, and it was only French insistence in February 1917 that resulted in coal ships sailing from England to France being convoyed. During the April crisis the French colliers were suffering a loss rate of 0.19 percent as against 25 percent elsewhere. Reluctantly the Admiralty allowed the first ocean convoy to sail at the end of April, and much to their surprise a miracle occurred: within a month the loss rate fell from 25 percent to 0.24 percent. By November 84,000 ships had been convoyed, of which only 257 were sunk.

For the U-Boats' convoy meant the end of easy pickings, for they could no longer lie in wait for whatever ship might come along. When smoke was seen on the horizon it heralded the arrival of 10 to 20 merchantmen surrounded by destroyers, sloops and patrol vessels, and often accompanied by an airship. All the U-Boat commanders' reports bear out the fact that the seas suddenly emptied, and an important side-effect was that U-Boats could no longer rely on the gun as a cheap and quick means of sinking ships. Now it was numbers of torpedoes carried which determined the endurance of a U-Boat, and this alone helped to reduce the tonnage sunk.

The British and their Allies took the offensive against the

Above: U-Boats accounted for the majority of their victims with gunfire in World War I.
Above right: A UB I boat cruises on the surface, showing how small these 'tin torpedoes' were.
Below: British Auxiliary Patrol trawlers stand by a torpedoed merchantman in 1918.

U-Boats in 1917, using a new type of horned mine modelled on the high lethal German 'egg' mine with its electro-chemical Herz horn. Using information gained from cryptanalysis, destroyer-minelayers and submarines laid mines in the exit-routes from Heligoland and Flanders. As soon as a new route was selected for the U-Boats the minelayers would promptly mine it, and in this way the minelaying UC-Boats operating out of

Flanders were finally neutralized. In 1918 an even more sinister weapon was introduced, the first magnetic mine.

The U-Boats kept up the pressure until the end, but the combination of convoy and other measures prevented them from ever getting back to the position that they had enjoyed in April 1917. When the Armistice was signed in November 1918 one of its most important clauses related to the U-Boats, all of which had to be surrendered in Allied ports. The German Navy had built some 360 submarines during the war, and a further 400 had either been cancelled or lay incomplete in the shipyards. The U-Boat Arm sank over 11 million tons of shipping and damaged a further 7½ million tons, but to achieve this 178 U-Boats were lost, and 5364 officers and men, nearly 40 percent of personnel.

FORCING THE DARDANELLES

After the first timid beginning the submarine war in the Mediterranean took a new turn with the Anglo-French attack on the Dardanelles. The Allies could not get surface warships through the Straits, and so looked to their submarines to achieve something, while the Germans felt that they ought to make some effort to help their new Turkish allies.

The only submarines available were three old British 'B' Class boats and the French *Brumaire* and *Circé*, which had all been sent to the Dardanelles at the end of 1914 to help maintain the blockade of the Dardanelles. On 1 December *B.11* left on a perilous journey up the Straits to see if a submarine could breast the 4–5 knot current and dive through the five rows of mines known to exist at Chanak (Cannakale). She had an exciting passage through the Narrows but she was rewarded by finding the old armored cruiser *Messudieh* lying at anchor, apparently safe from attack. A single 18-inch torpedo was enough to sink the target, hardly an outstanding victory but one to offset the recent successes of the U-Boats in the North Sea.

As a direct result of *B.11*'s exploit the British and French sent more modern submarines to the Dardanelles and their arrival coincided with the Allied landings. The Anglo-French offensive was not going well and any interference with the Turks' supply-routes through the Sea of Marmora would benefit the hard pressed troops at Gallipoli. But forcing the Dardanelles was still very dangerous, even for a modern submarine.

The *E.15* tried it and ran aground, followed by the French *Saphir*; the Australian *AE.2* got through on 26 April only to be sunk, but her sister *E.14* followed her a day later. The French *Joule* was mined on 1 May, making the loss rate four submarines for every one that arrived in the sea of Marmora. But when the news got through that *E.14* had sunk three ships the Allies redoubled their efforts, and soon another six British submarines and the French *Turquoise* reached the Sea of Marmora.

The German *U.21* under Kapitänleutnant Hersing had also made a safe passage of the Dardanelles from Cattaro. Six of the small UB-Boats and four UC-Boats were sent to the Adriatic by rail to be reassembled at Cattaro, and three of the UB-Boats were sent to the Dardanelles to join Hersing at Constantinople. Two arrived safely but it was *U.21* which scored the first success. On 25 May Hersing spotted the old battleship *Triumph* firing at Turkish positions near Gaba Tepe. He had to wait two hours for a favorable shot, but when it came a single torpedo sent the *Triumph* down. Two days later he came upon another old battleship, HMS *Majestic* off Cape Helles, at anchor. She was surrounded by colliers and patrol vessels, but the man who had waited two hours to get the *Triumph* was not easily put off, and eventually a gap opened. Again a single torpedo sufficed to send the *Majestic* over on her beam ends. The obsolescence of the ships was immaterial; they had been sunk in full view of the troops fighting ashore and Hersing's feat was therefore all the more

Above: A view of the interior of the German submarine *Deutschland* showing the control room.
Below: *U.35*, the command of the 'ace' Arnauld de la Perière, about to submerge.

dramatic. The bombarding ships had to be withdrawn to Mudros, and at a crucial moment the presence of *U.21* put fresh heart into the Turkish troops.

Italy joined the war on the side of the Allies on 24 May 1915. Her large surface fleet offered the Austrian and German U-Boats tempting targets, but as she had only declared war on Austria the German submariners at Cattaro were in a difficult situation. The solution was a simple one; the German boats pretended to be Austrian until such time as Italy chose to include Germany among her enemies. *UB.15* and *UB.1* were among the boats reassembled at Cattaro, and they were nominally commissioned as *X* and *XI*, (in October 1915 the Austro-Hungarian Navy adopted the U-prefix with Arabic numerals). Among their successes in the Adriatic were the sinkings of the Italian submarines *Medusa* and *Nereide* and the armored cruisers *Amalfi* and *Giuseppe Garibaldi*.

The five small U-Boats sent to Turkey had been formed into a half-flotilla under Otto Hersing as senior officer. Her pursued a vigorous policy in the Black Sea and in the Sea of Marmora but had too few boats to deal with the Russian Fleet as well as the Allied submarines in the Sea of Marmora. The British submarines' campaign against the Turks is a classic of economy of effort, for a handful of submarines was able to dominate both land and sea communications for eight months. It was discovered that trains could be bombarded with deck-guns, and so British submarines followed the German trend towards heavier

guns. The campaign only ended in January 1916 when the Allies evacuated the Gallipoli Peninsula, but in that time submarines had virtually stopped all seaborne communication between Istanbul and the Gallipoli Peninsula.

The Mediterranean remained a good hunting ground for U-Boats right to the end. Some of their most notable successes were scored there, including the torpedoing of the battleships HMS *Cornwallis* and the French *Danton*. The introduction of convoy in 1917 brought the losses under control just as rapidly as it did in the Atlantic.

If British submarine operations in the North Sea were humdrum the same could not be said about the Baltic, where they equalled their achievements in the Sea of Marmora. The situation was similar to that in the Dardanelles: Russia was under pressure from the German Navy as well as on land, and any diversionary effort by the Royal Navy would reduce some of the strain. In October 1914, therefore, two 'E' Class submarines left their East Coast base bound for the Baltic via the Kattegat. Their port of destination was Libau (now Liepaja) but when the two boats arrived they found a scene of utter confusion. The Russians were blowing up ammunition and port installations before evacuating Libau in the face of the advancing German armies. The submarines were given a new base at Lapvik in the Gulf of Finland, and here they were able to repair the minor damage and wear and tear before getting down to business.

The Western Baltic was virtually a German lake, and it was used for training by the High Seas Fleet. The first boat, *E.1* had already fired at the cruiser *Viktoria Luise* but missed; *E.9* was more successful when she sank the destroyer *S.120* off Kiel. However, German warships were not the prime targets for the

Below: The Italian steamer SS *Stromboli* sinking in the Mediterranean in a picture taken from the attacking submarine.

Above: The salvaged hull of *UC.5* seen in dry dock at Harwich, showing her mine chutes.

two submarines, but rather the merchant ships carrying iron ore from Sweden. The Germans were soon convinced that a whole flotilla of boats was operating, and even convinced themselves that a mysterious depot ship was operating in the Western Baltic. In August 1915 the first reinforcements arrived at Lapvik. In addition four of the old 'C' Class were sent as deck cargo to Arkhangelsk, and then by canal barge and rail all the way down to Lapvik where they were reassembled.

By October 1915 the nine British submarines were ready to resume the offensive, and with the help of Russian submarines they inflicted heavy losses. But after the Menshevik or 'February' Revolution in March 1917 the efficiency of the base-support at Lapvik declined steadily. When the Bolsheviks signed the Treaty of Brest-Litovsk they agreed to surrender the British submarines to the Germans, but this the British would not allow at any price. On 8 April 1918 one of the few Russian ships which was still 'friendly' forced a passage to allow the submarines to reach open sea. By this time the seven survivors were based at Helsingfors (now Helsinki) and once they reached deep water scuttling charges were detonated.

By the end of the First World War the submarine had undergone much the same sort of transformation as the aircraft. From being a rather quaint instrument of limited potential it blossomed into a most advanced and complex weapon. Its special requirements acted as a spur to industry to improve every item of its equipment, the diesel engine, the periscope and the torpedo to name only three. Its unexpected flexibility as a weapon changed the nature of sea warfare completely. The British admirals at the Battle of Jutland could not maneuver freely through fear of being torpedoed by submarines. Their depredations among the world's merchant fleets in 1915–17 nearly bankrupted the British Empire, and certainly hastened its decline, but it had other side-effects. One of their saddest achievements was the virtual extinction of the sailing ship, many of which had been trading profitably in 1914. The blockade of Germany and the U-Boat campaign between them inflicted near-starvation and malnutrition on poor people in both Britain and Germany, and even neutral Europe suffered from the widespread food shortage. Even today the ruthlessness of U-Boat warfare raises a shudder, but in fairness we must admire the courage of the men who took their small submarines to sea in all weathers. Submarine warfare was and will always be a mixture of bravery and utter ruthlessness.

WOLFPACKS UNLEASHED

When World War II began on the morning of 3 September 1939 both British and German submarines were already at their war stations. The Royal Navy had eight boats based at Dundee, six at Blyth, and a further 16 on training duties, in addition to a pair of old boats being brought forward from reserve, five in the Mediterranean and 15 in the Far East. The Germans had sent 21 U-Boats to sea with the pocket battleships *Deutschland* and *Graf Spee* a month earlier. Their boats were based on Kiel (25 boats divided between four flotillas), 17 boats in two flotillas at Wilhelmshaven and 12 boats for training at Neustadt. The French Navy's Division des Sous-Marins (DSM) had also alerted its flotillas; apart from submarines abroad there were 28 boats based on Toulon, 17 at Bizerta and 12 at Casablanca.

Both sides were wary, and the Germans in particular had strict orders not to deviate from the Prize Regulations. It may seem mildly quixotic of Hitler to insist on the observance of such rules after violating almost every other rule of international law but he was well aware of how important it was to give American opinion no opportunity to turn against Germany. The results were ludicrous, all the more so because the chief beneficiaries of this policy, the British, did not even expect it to be followed. British Merchant Navy captains had been instructed to the effect that a 'sink at sight' policy would be followed immediately, and were told to ignore the Prize Regulations. Yet most U-Boat captains made an effort to carry out their orders. When Kapitänleutnant Lemp, in *U.30* identified the liner *Athenia* wrongly as a troopship he reported his mistake to Admiral Dönitz, who promptly threatened him with a court martial. Unfortunately the Propaganda Ministry then took a hand, accusing the Royal Navy and Winston Churchill of sabotaging the *Athenia* to discredit Germany and to support this story the U-Boat's logbook and other material evidence was suppressed. Some commanders, like Herbert Schultze in *U.48* went so far as to send messages 'in clear' to the British to give them positions of lifeboats.

Even when the U-Boats were restrained in their attacks on Allied shipping they sank 114 ships totalling 421,156 tons between 3 September and 31 December 1939. The Prize Regulations were held not to apply in the North Sea from the end of September, and on 2 October U-Boats were given permission to attack any ship sailing without lights off either the British or French coasts. On 4 October the exemption from the Prize Regulations was extended to longitude 15 degrees West and two weeks later U-Boats were given permission to attack all ships identified as hostile. The last prohibition, forbidding attacks on liners was removed on 17 November and unrestricted submarine warfare was back.

The most spectacular U-Boat successes were, however, against warships in these first weeks of the war. On 12 Septem-

Above: The Type VIIB *U.101* comes alongside a tender.
Left: A heavily retouched view of the secret *K.21*, which claimed to have torpedoed the *Tirpitz*.
Far left: *U.557* with an interned Dutch liner.
Below: The British *Syrtis* off Liverpool, 1943.

ber *U.29* sank the aircraft carrier HMS *Courageous* which was ironically on antisubmarine patrol in the Western Approaches. A large, fast warship is not an easy target for any submarine, and Kapitänleutnant Schuhart had to wait for nearly two hours before the carrier turned into wind to allow her aircraft to land. Had the *Courageous* not detached two of her four destroyers to help a sinking merchant ship *U.29* might still have been frustrated in her attack, but Schuhart was too skilled a submariner

to let the chance slip, and at 1950 three torpedoes tore into the ship and sent her down with the loss of more than 500 men. Two days later the new carrier *Ark Royal* had a lucky escape west of the Hebrides, when she was missed by torpedoes which passed astern. This time the destroyers detected *U.39* on Asdic and sank her with depth charges, but it was clear to the Admiralty that big fleet carriers could not be hazarded on such dangerous work, and they were withdrawn.

Exactly one month later Günther Prien in *U.47* achieved one of the most outstanding submarine exploits of all time. Knowing from aerial reconnaissance that the winter gales had opened gaps in the blockships which had been sunk in one of the eastern entrances to Scapa Flow, the U-Boat Command gave permission for an attempt to penetrate the defences. Prien was undertaking a mission fraught with danger but his courage was rewarded when he found himself in the Flow. The main anchorage was empty because most of the Home Fleet was no longer there, but to the North Prien found the old battleship *Royal Oak*. He fired a bow salvo of three torpedoes, and was mortified to hear only a small explosion, so slight that people aboard the battleship thought it was either a collision or an internal explosion. Prien turned to fire his stern tube at the battleship but missed, and was forced to reload his forward tubes. This time all three torpedoes ran true and exploded underneath the *Royal Oak*'s hull, and 13 minutes later the 25-year old veteran of the Battle of

Left: British 'T' Class boats in the Gareloch.
Right: *U.561* passes through a lock gate in the Kiel Canal heading for the North Sea.
Below right: *U.558* lies in dry dock under camouflage netting.
Below: Günther Prien aboard *U.47*.

Jutland rolled over suddenly and sank, taking 833 officers and men with her.

However elderly and out-of-date the *Royal Oak* might be, her loss was a blow to the Royal Navy's prestige and a reminder that the Home Fleet's main base was not properly protected. The Home Fleet was forced to move to Loch Ewe on the west coast of Scotland, in precisely the same manner as the Grand Fleet had been dispersed in 1914. Once again a single submarine had brought about a major shift of surface fleets and affected seriously the conduct of operations at sea. At a crucial moment the Home Fleet had to move away from its theater of operations and so leave the vital exit route to the Atlantic unguarded. But the German Navy was in no better a position to exploit its victory than it had been 25 years before, and the chance was lost again.

The Admiralty suffered no doubts about convoy such as they had in 1917, and drew up elaborate plans for the immediate convoying of merchant ships. All that was lacking was sufficient escorts, and to economize on warships for this purpose 'close'

Left: *U.557*'s 10.5cm gun undergoes maintenance.
Right: HM Submarine *Shark* surrendered to German trawlers in the Kattegat in 1940.
Below: The *Shcha* Class of boat was one of the more successful Soviet designs.
Bottom: The famous Free French submarine *Rubis*, 1946.

escort was not provided for convoys further west than 15 degrees. In coastal waters constant aircraft patrols were effective in keeping the U-Boats under control, and when the new coastal escorts or Flower Class corvettes began to come into service in the spring of 1940 they proved very effective. To avoid this concentration of counter-measures the U-Boats moved further west, and as a result the convoy escort limit had to be moved out to 17 degrees West in July, and again to 19 degrees West from October 1940. Similarly on the other side of the Atlantic the Canadians had to extend their convoy limit from 56 degrees to 53½ degrees West, but in between was the 'Black-Gap' in which merchant ships had neither air nor surface escorts. However, the U-Boats were still far from winning an outright victory because of their own shortage of numbers; many had to be retained for training, others were refitting between patrols, and sinkings by British antisubmarine forces were keeping abreast of new construction.

The respite gave the hard-pressed British and French navies time to develop their convoy organisation and to complete and convert more escort vessels. In addition deep minefields were laid in the English Channel to block it to U-Boats and so force them to use precious fuel and time on the northern passage to the Western Approaches. In the previous war the Dover Barrage had taken four years to perfect, but this time it worked completely; only one U-Boat got through and three others were mined in the first month.

British submarines were active in the North Sea, but the absence of major targets meant that they could do little more than watch or try to attack the occasional U-Boat on passage. The principal bases for these operations were Blyth and Dundee on the East coast of Scotland, but in October 1939 the Admiralty decided to concentrate the submarines temporarily at Rosyth until they could be better defended against air attack. They were reinforced by two Polish boats, the *Wilk* and *Orzel* which had escaped from the Baltic after the defeat of Poland. Another

base was established at Harwich, using the new 3rd Flotilla, created from boats withdrawn from the Mediterranean.

The British flotillas got their chance for action with the opening of the Norwegian Campaign in April 1940. The British Government was anxious about the extent to which German ships were taking iron ore from Norwegian ports. Although the traffic itself was perfectly legal the German ore-ships were able to take full advantage of Norway's military weakness by infringing her neutrality in a number of minor ways. The British finally reached a decision to lay a 'declared' minefield (that is one whose area and extent were notified to all neutrals)

Above: Ratings stow torpedoes in the forward torpedo room of a British submarine.
Below: A 'T' Class submarine enters harbor.

Above left: A censored view of HMS *Sturgeon* arriving home in 1940 after sinking a German transport.
Above: A Soviet sailor works on a torpedo.

as a retaliation for German breaches of Norwegian neutrality. This move coincided with Hitler's decision to occupy Norway to forestall the British invasion that he felt was inevitable. The result was that British and German naval forces encountered one another in a state of mutual ignorance and surprise.

The first intimation of what was afoot came when the Polish submarine *Orzel* sank a German transport off Christansand at noon on 8 April. Yet, although soldiers picked up by Norwegian craft admitted that they were on their way to occupy Bergen, and in spite of this news reaching the Admiralty that evening, nothing was done to alert the other submarines in position. Even when the submarines were given the vital information they were hamstrung by the same Prize Regulations as had hampered the U-Boats earlier. Even to the British Cabinet such hair-splitting was finally unacceptable; Allied submarines were given permission to sink transports on 9 April, and two days after that they were freed to attack any ship sighted up to ten miles from the Norwegian coast.

The results were spectacular and in less than a month 18 transports, tankers and other mercantile vessels were sunk, as well as the cruiser *Karlsruhe*, the gunnery training ship *Brummer* and a U-Boat. In addition submarine-laid mines accounted for another 13 ships, and the 'pocket battleship' *Lutzow* was badly damaged by HMS *Spearfish*. The losses were not unduly heavy, considering that nearly 100,000 tons of scarce German shipping had been sunk; 3 boats were sunk and one lost in a collision.

By comparison the U-Boats did not do well. The magnetic pistols for their torpedoes were adversely affected by an unforeseen change in the Earth's magnetism in the high latitudes off Norway, and so U-Boat commanders were robbed of a number of targets. Most of the U-Boats had been withdrawn from the Atlantic for the campaign, and so the resulting lull took the pressure off the Royal Navy at a crucial time, with nothing to compensate for it elsewhere.

While the Germans were consolidating their gains in Norway their main armies were preparing to invade France and the Low Countries. As soon as news of the German invasion of Belgium was heard on 10 May the bulk of the Allied submarine force was withdrawn from Norway, leaving only the British *Severn* and *Clyde*, the Polish *Orzel* and the French *Rubis* to harrass the Germans. All other submarines were redeployed to prevent German surface forces from making any incursion into the southern North Sea in support of their land forces.

The fall of first Holland and then France meant that Dutch and French submarines fled to British ports. Strenuous efforts were made to get submarines out of Brest and Cherbourg, and in some cases submarines completing refits or even still under construction were towed away. In all the giant *Surcouf* and six smaller submarines reached England.

Above: *U.558* lies camouflaged in dock to avoid the incessant Allied air raids.
Right: The Soviet *D.2* at Polyarnoe, near Murmansk.

But under the armistice conditions agreed by Marshal Pétain, French naval officers were ordered to take their ships back to France, where they would be kept out of German hands. Not unnaturally the British, knowing just how valuable the French Navy would be to make good the deficiencies of the *Kriegsmarine*, doubted that the French would be allowed to keep their end of the bargain. After Dunkirk the British Government knew that it was fighting for survival, nothing less, and feeling that it dared not gamble once again on a written agreement, took over all French warships lying in British ports.

Within hours of the fall of France Admiral Dönitz and his staff were ready with plans to exploit the situation. Road transport was commandeered to move heavy equipment such as air compressors and torpedoes from Germany down to the French Atlantic coast. From Lorient, Bordeaux, Brest, St Nazaire, La Rochelle and La Pallice, U-Boats could now reach

Left: Ratings man the Finch gun aboard a British 'S' Class boat.
Below: The 'T' Class submarines had two 21 inch torpedo tubes beneath the conning tower, but these were later resited.

Left: A U-Boat in dry dock displays the knife-edged lines of its hull.
Below: An ensign flutters above a surfaced U-Boat.
Bottom: A U-Boat's hull is examined for damage.
Far right: A U-Boat's lookouts scan the horizon as the boat runs on the surface.
Below far right: U-Boat crew members parade for inspection.

the densely crowded shipping routes in the Atlantic quickly, and so could spend more time on patrol. It was a profound change in the naval situation, for the U-Boats had completely out-flanked their opponents; to make matters worse the British had lost the use of the greater part of the French Navy and the large French mercantile marine. To add to their problems the Italians had entered the War, and in August 1940 they set up a submarine base at Bordeaux. By the beginning of 1941 this base could support 27 submarines.

The new distribution of U-Boats in the Atlantic comprised eight flotillas, all under Operation Area West, at Brest. The other flotillas were distributed in Germany (4th and 5th) and Norway (11th and 13th).

Had the Italian submarines been better suited to Atlantic conditions their reinforcement of the U-Boats might have been decisive, but they achieved comparatively little. Operating mainly off the Azores, they sank about 1,000,000 tons of shipping between January 1941 and September 1943. This was an average of approximately 31,000 tons sunk by each of the 32 boats involved; by comparison the 14 Type IXB U-Boats which operated in roughly the same area sank 40 percent more. But the U-Boats also suffered from problems. The Type VII U-Boat was found to be on the small side for operating so far out into the Atlantic, and special 'milch-cow' U-tankers were designed, which could transfer diesel fuel and spare torpedoes to other U-Boats at sea. Only ten of these underwater supply vessels were completed in 1941–42, and as all were made the object of special attention by Allied antisubmarine forces they were all early losses. The big Type IX boats had more endurance, but their bulk and slow diving made them particularly vulnerable in the Western Approaches. They were mostly employed away from the main convoy routes, where the escorts were less active and many of their victims were unescorted. Largely because of this the IXB Class accounted for approximately 10 percent of the entire mercantile tonnage sunk by U-Boats.

Between June and November 1940 British and neutral shipping losses from U-Boats rose to 1,600,000 tons. This was the heyday of a new generation of 'ace' U-Boat commanders, men like Otto Kretschmer and Günther Prien, who sank more than 200,000 tons apiece. Kretschmer in *U.99* was the leading exponent of a brilliant new tactic, the night attack on the surface. Taking advantage of her low silhouette and relatively high speed on her diesel motors, a U-Boat could actually penetrate the columns of a convoy of merchant ships undetected, from which position her CO could fire his torpedoes with impunity. The escort commanders were usually on the flanks of the convoy, and unless an exceptionally alert lookout, watching in the least likely quarter, happened to spot the trimmed down conning tower, the chances of detection were slim. Radar put an end to this practice, but in 1940 no convoy escort had a radar set, and the only answer was to provide artificial illuminating rockets known as Snowflakes, which could act like starshell and turn night into day.

Even the efforts of the 'aces' were not enough for Admiral Dönitz. Realizing that there would never be time to train a new generation of commanders of the quality of Kretschmer, Schepke and the others, he developed a concept which had been suggested over twenty years earlier by Commodore Bauer. This was the mass-attack or 'wolf-pack' idea (German *Rudeltaktik*), in which a force of 20 or more U-Boats could swamp a convoy's defences. Briefly the sequence of a wolf-pack attack would be as follows:

1. A pack of U-Boats is disposed in a wide curve across the probable route of a convoy.
2. Any U-Boat sighting the convoy signals its course, speed and composition, as well as its own position to U-Boat HQ.
3. The U-Boat then shadows the convoy without attacking, and merely reports any change in course and speed.
4. U-Boat HQ orders all other U-Boats in the pack to make contact with U-Boat No. 1.
5. When all U-Boats have made contact with the shadower a coordinated attack is made on the convoy after dark.
6. At daybreak the pack breaks off the attack leaving one shadower to maintain contact, while the others recharge batteries and load fresh torpedoes.
7. At nightfall the pack renews its attack.

The wolf-pack system had the advantage that it made the best use of the newly trained and relatively inexperienced U-Boat captains and crews, and inevitably it wrought havoc among the poorly escorted convoys of 1940. The new methods were introduced gradually between October 1940 and March 1941, but by then the British had in any case scored such success against the aces that it became obvious to Dönitz that pack-tactics were the only effective method left.

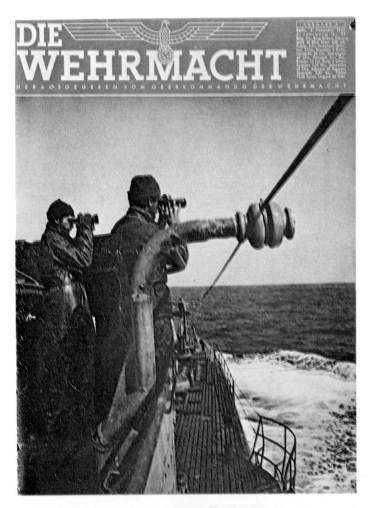

In March 1941 the escorts got Prien in *U.47*, and then Schepke in *U.100* and Kretschmer in *U.99*, all sunk while attacking convoys. It was a heavy blow to the U-Boat Arm, for these three men alone had sunk 111 ships totalling over half a million tons. They had fallen victim to the new weapons and techniques of convoy escort, for the British had introduced surface search radar, radio direction-finding and a series of new weapons and tactics. There were two great weaknesses in the wolf-pack system: all depended on the shadower and on communications between U-Boat HQ and the pack, and if any means could be discovered of hindering either of these the defenders could hold their own.

The simplest means of dealing with shadowers was to maintain an aircraft patrol astern of the convoy, so that the shadowing U-Boat was forced to dive, and could therefore no longer keep up. The most urgent need, therefore, was to provide air cover for convoys all the way across the Atlantic, but until the end of 1941 there were neither the aircraft nor the aircraft carriers to spare for this. In mid-1941 the Admiralty began to convert an experimental escort carrier, a small merchant ship with an extemporized wooden flight deck, but she was not ready until the end of the year. In 1917–18 Allied cryptographers had eavesdropped on the large volume of radio traffic between the U-Boats and their bases, but in 1940–41 German codes and cyphers were secure against this. However, the source could be located by a sufficiently sensitive high-frequency receiver. Unknown to the Germans, the British were successful in producing a set small enough to be fitted in a small warship; using it, an escort could pinpoint the position of a U-Boat to within a quarter of a mile, and so escorts could drive off shadowers or even sink them.

When a corvette went to sea in May 1941 with the first Type 271 surface warning radar set she was able to detect a conning tower at night at 2½ miles. This was the countermeasure which enabled escorts to deal with night attacks at last, and it was put into quantity production immediately. In May 1941 a British boarding party captured code-books and an Enigma cypher machine intact from *U.110* before she sank, probably the greatest intelligence 'pinch' of the War. Hitherto the German B-Dienst or cryptographic service had enjoyed considerable success in locating convoys, but as soon as the secrets of the *U.110* haul were unravelled the advantage passed to the other side.

In 1941 a number of new antisubmarine weapons were introduced. At last an efficient aerial depth-charge was available, and ships were given extra-heavy depth-charges designed to sink faster. The standard Asdic set could not hold a submarine in its beam directly underneath, and so contact was lost in the final moments of an attack. To remedy this the Hedgehog ahead-throwing weapon was devised to hurl 24 small bombs in a pattern forward, while the escort still held the U-Boat in contact. Despite all these countermeasures 1941 saw the loss of more than 2,000,000 tons of shipping, 432 ships in all. The British, even allowing for the neutral nations' shipping which was available, could not stand losses of this order. The German attack on Russia in mid-1941 did little to ease the situation because the Russians were in no position to offer any naval assistance or draw off any substantial number of U-Boats. All now depended on the Americans, who alone could provide the shipping to offset the huge losses inflicted by the U-Boats.

The attitude of the United States had been pro-Allied right from the start of the War, but of course as a neutral she could not lend direct support to any belligerent. However, President Franklin Roosevelt was resolved to offer 'all aid short of war,' and had already lent the British 50 old destroyers for escort purposes in return for base-rights in British colonial possessions. The later Lend-Lease Act of March 1941 was a fiction to allow war material to be made available 'on loan' to Britain but however it might enrage Hitler, his orders to Admiral Dönitz were to avoid provoking the Americans into a declaration of war. In September 1941 the US President went a step further and ordered the US Navy to escort American merchant ships bound for the British Isles to a Mid-Ocean Meeting Point, (MOMP) and warships were given orders to attack any submarines which appeared to be attacking American ships. As the meeting point was near Iceland, where British escort vessels were based, it was not long before incidents occurred between U-Boats and American ships.

On 4 September the old destroyer USS *Greer* picked up a submarine contact on her Sonar (the USN equivalent of Asdic), and following standard orders tracked and shadowed it without making an attack. But the *Greer* was broadcasting in clear and soon a British shore-based aircraft arrived and dropped depth-charges. Under the impression that the *Greer* had attacked him, the CO of *U.652* lost his patience, ignored his orders and fired a torpedo at the destroyer. Although it missed the *Greer*, she went to action stations and counterattacked, but without success. The next incident was on 10 October, when a U-Boat torpedoed the US destroyer *Kearny*, whose silhouette was very similar to the British escort destroyers operating in the area. The *Kearny* did not sink but the attack whipped up anti-German feeling to a new pitch. Worse was to follow, for on 31 October the old destroyer *Reuben James* was sunk, but still the United States was so reluctant to get involved in World War II that President

Top: Lookouts on *U.86*'s conning tower.
Above: The French boat *Circé*.
Above right: The view from a U-Boat's 21cm gun platform.
Below: *U.27* was photographed from *U.26* during a prewar training cruise.

Roosevelt could do nothing but express his indignation. For his part Hitler was adamant in his decision to avoid hostilities with America, and refused to lift the restrictions on the U-Boats. The undeclared war continued without further major incidents until the Japanese attack on Pearl Harbor on 7 December. Two days later Hitler removed all restrictions on attacks against American shipping, and two days after that declared war on the United States. The Battle of the Atlantic was about to enter an even fiercer stage.

MEDITERRANEAN LIFELINES

The Italian Navy had built a large force of submarines before the outbreak of war, and the Italian High Command or *Supermarina* had high hopes of denying the British the use of their main base, Malta. With some 90 submarines at their disposal and being very close to Malta, they should have been a decisive factor in the naval war but in fact it was the British submarines which took this honor from them.

When Italy declared war on France and Great Britain in June 1940, the British were in the process of reforming their submarine flotillas after withdrawing all but two submarines for training. With boats transferred from China it was possible to base six at Alexandria and six at Malta, but none could be spared for Gibraltar. The boats sent were too large for the Mediterranean and before the end of the first two weeks of operations the *Grampus*, the *Odin* and *Orpheus* were lost. Visibility in Mediterranean waters is so good that an aircraft can spot a submarine 50 feet down in calm weather, and the fact that the three submarines had recently come from China could have meant that their COs had not yet learned how to cope with these difficult conditions. Another factor may have been the tendency for the British 'O' Class boats to disclose their positions by fuel leaks from their saddle tanks outside the pressure hull.

The Italian lines of communication in the Mediterranean were vulnerable to submarine attack, and the dangers had to be taken into account if the British were to offset their numerical inferiority in surface ships. The targets were mainly the shipping carrying men and supplies to the North African colonies, but it was not until February 1941 that British submarines were allowed to attack all shipping at sight. In spite of this handicap and poor aerial reconnaissance the British submarine flotillas sank a number of transports and warships, for the loss of one French and nine British boats. During the same period Italian submarines achieved very few successes, and sank no warships at all. The reasons for this failure were partly the transfer of most of the top Italian submarines to France and partly the design of the boats themselves, which were also too large and clumsy for Mediterranean operations.

In many ways the campaign resembled the 1915 campaign in the Sea of Marmora, with the gun being used as much as the torpedo. Submarines were used to land raiding parties and to bombard shore targets such as trains. In the early part of 1941 British land forces were doing well against the Italians in North Africa, and the depredations of the Malta submarines added to the problems of the *Regia Navale* in escorting supply-convoys. But when the *Luftwaffe* came to the rescue of the Italians they were able to make life much harder for British submarines. Aircraft minelaying caused losses, and heavy air attacks on Malta made it almost untenable as a base. Losses were heavy, but the Axis armies were seriously hampered by the attacks on their supply-lines. Between January and May 1941 the Germans and Italians lost 100,000 tons of shipping to submarines alone, nearly a third of their total losses to surface and air attack, mines and other causes. Between June and September they lost another 150,000 tons, but the total fell to half that figure between October and December reflecting the reversal of British fortunes in the Mediterranean. The Italian merchant fleet was reduced by 30 percent in a year, a rate of decline which would eventually prove disastrous for the Axis position in the Mediterranean.

Until the autumn of 1941 there were no U-Boats in the Mediterranean as Admiral Dönitz refused to allow any of his precious boats to be withdrawn from the Battle of the Atlantic. He rightly felt that the war would be won or lost in the Atlantic, and maintained that the Italians should have been capable of looking after the Mediterranean by themselves. But the successes of the British Mediterranean Fleet and the ceaseless harrying of convoys by the Malta submarines threatened to bring about the collapse of the Italians, and so Hitler over-ruled Dönitz. During September six U-Boats left the Biscay ports, and another four passed successfully through the Straits of Gibraltar in October. Dönitz was resigned to losing them permanently, for the eastward current and thermal layers in the Straits which made it relatively easy for a submarine to get into the Mediterranean made it correspondingly hazardous to get out again.

All the U-Boats were eventually hunted down, as Dönitz had foreseen, but they gave a good account of themselves. On 13 November *U.81* sank the famous *Ark Royal* near Gibraltar and so robbed the Gibraltar forces of their only carrier. On 25 November the battleship *Barham* was torpedoed by *U.331*, and blew up with the loss of 862 officers and men. As Admiral Cunningham ruefully commented, the British antisubmarine forces had become a little rusty as a result of only having to deal with Italian submarines, and the U-Boat managed to get right through the Battle Fleet's destroyer-screen without being detected.

British submarines suffered heavily in the summer of 1942, for they were operating in areas almost entirely dominated by hostile air power. Many were sunk and others were damaged in harbor. Malta's situation became so precarious that the submarines had to supply the garrison with such diverse stores as high octane gasoline, kerosene, machine-gun ammunition and glycol coolant for Spitfires. The use of submarines for this vital purpose had started in May 1941, and in some cases conversion involved the removal of one battery to provide more space. It was the big minelayers like the *Rorqual* which carried cargo most easily on their capacious mine-decks, but the *Clyde* carried 1200 tons on one trip. All in all some 65,000 tons of supplies were landed by submarines before the crisis was over. Even so the submarines were forced to lie on the bottom of the harbor during daylight, and could only surface at night. Every submarine engaged on supply-runs was a submarine not available for attacking Italian and German supply ships; it is quite clear from German records that submarines accounted for over half the tonnage of shipping sunk in the first half of 1942, and that those losses rose after Malta was relieved by the big Pedestal convoy action in August and after the Battle of El Alamein brought the coast of North Africa under Allied control once more.

Above: The *Sturgeon* returns to Dundee, September 1940.
Right: *U.505* is preserved at Chicago, Illinois.
Below right: *U.995* is today preserved at Laboe, outside Kiel in West Germany. This view shows the boat's forward torpedo room.
Bottom: The control room of the preserved *U.995*.
Below: The Italian wartime submarine *Marcello* is pictured in harbor.

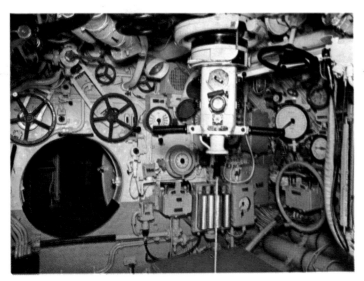

THE BLACK GAP

Hitler's declaration of war on the United States in December 1941 came as no surprise to the U-Boat High Command for Admiral Dönitz and his staff felt that it was inevitable. Plans were ready for Operation Drumroll or *Paukenschlag*, and by 25 December six U-Boats were on their way across the Atlantic to attack American shipping.

The US Navy had been in close touch with the Royal Navy, and all reports on antisubmarine tactics and equipment were available. Yet the fierceness of *Paukenschlag* took the USN completely by surprise and an amazing lack of preparedness led to the loss of 500 ships in the first six months. U-Boat commanders had referred to the period June–December 1940 as the 'happy time,' and now they rejoiced at the return of the happy time as they slaughtered ships sailing independently. Destroyers steamed in every direction on 'offensive' patrols, so regularly that they could be timed by the U-Boats, ships broadcast their positions in clear and shore lights gave the U-Boats easy navigational bearings. The US Navy had been suspicious of the efficacy of convoy, despite its deep involvement in the defeat of the U-Boat offensive in 1917–18, and some senior officers felt that the task of escorting a convoy plodding along at 10 knots was too humdrum. It might be right for the stolid British and Canadian character but it did not suit the more dashing American temperament, or so it was claimed. Attractive though this line of reasoning might be it was totally wrong. Nor was it unique to the Americans; it had been used frequently between 1915 and 1917 by the British to prove that convoy was too defensive a measure for a navy inbred with the Nelson spirit. More important, developments in Sonar had not kept pace with

the British Asdic, and considerable leeway had to be made up quickly by the US Navy. Although the need for special escort vessels had been foreseen, financial limitations had prevented the Navy from placing any orders, but fortunately the British had already placed an order for destroyer-escorts (DEs) under Lend-Lease. The programme was immediately expanded from 50 to 250 DEs, and it was possible for the Royal Navy to transfer 25 corvettes as a temporary measure. The British had also designed a new escort vessel specially for the North Atlantic, the 'River' Class High Endurance Escort (later called the frigate), and an American copy was put into production. All these measures took time, and all the while the U-Boats were adding to their scores.

During 1942 the monthly average shipping loss was 650,000 tons, and in that year the U-Boats sank 6 million tons. By December Admiral Dönitz had 212 U-Boats operational, and the war was entering a critical phase. In simple strategic terms the U-Boats could cut the United States off from Great Britain and the Mediterranean, and so make it impossible for her to bring her vast resources to bear anywhere in the European Theater. If this had happened, and Dönitz estimated that a monthly average loss of 800,000 tons of shipping would do it, not even the wealth and industrial might of America would have been any use to her. She might have been able to deal with Japan in the Pacific, but her entire Eastern Seaboard would have been vulnerable to seaborne attack. Thus the Battle of the Atlantic came to mean much more than the survival of Great Britain; it was the decisive theater of the western half of World War II, and the victor would win the war.

There were several factors balancing the enormous losses of shipping. By mid-1942 the American shipyards were able to provide the first purpose-built escort carriers, and in the fall

Below: A Type VIIC U-Boat lashed by depth-charges and cannon fire sinks by the stern.

the first Very Long Range Liberator antisubmarine patrol air-craft came into service, and these measures did much to close the Black Gap by providing continuous air cover to convoys. British shipyards were also beginning to turn out larger num-bers of escort vessels, and it was possible to form the first Sup-port Groups in September of that year. These were groups of well-trained escorts, usually destroyers and frigates or sloops, which operated independently of the convoys to break up con-centrations of U-Boats and to harry them on passages to their patrol areas. If they sound suspiciously like the old discredited concept of offensive patrolling this is erroneous, for the support group supplemented the convoy system and was intended to reinforce any convoy that was hard-pressed, as well as hunting further afield. One of the drawbacks of convoying was that an escort which had detected a submarine was often forced to break off the attack prematurely in order to catch up with her convoy. The support group was free to spend hours or even days if needed on a lengthy hunt to destruction.

The climax of the Battle of the Atlantic might have come in the fall of 1942, for all the tactics and weaponry on both sides had been perfected, but political decisions at a high level resulted in the escort carriers and support groups being with-drawn to cover the Allied invasion of North Africa, Operation Torch. The U-Boats were not slow to take advantage of this weakening of the Allied effort in the Atlantic but the effect was delayed by the winter weather, which hampered the U-Boats as much as it did the escorts. Furthermore in the first two months of 1943 the Germans encountered difficulty in locating convoys, due to the Admiralty's success in rerouting convoys to avoid wolf-packs whose position was known.

The first big battle was in March, when two groups of U-Boats tried unsuccessfully to trap convoy SC-121. In a battle lasting five days 13 ships were sunk, despite the fact that the convoy slipped through the patrol line. Later that month, after the German B-Dienst cracked the current convoy cypher, Admiral Dönitz concentrated 40 U-Boats against the slow convoy SC-122

Above: A U-Boat puts to sea, getting the 'send off' which Admiral Dönitz knew was essential for morale.
Below: Two U-Boats are moored in their bomb-proof 'pen' at St Nazaire.
Bottom: The successful *U.48* takes on a torpedo.

Above: The conning tower and periscope details of *U.776* photographed in the London Docks after World War II.

a British navigator to the effect that the Metox receiver produced a signal which could be traced by Allied aircraft was sufficient to throw everybody off the scent. Convinced that the Metox was giving away the positions of the U-Boats, the Germans ordered all sets to be removed, whereas this offensive piece of equipment was simply incapable of detecting short waveband (10-cm) radar pulses.

A similar error had been made in 1942, when U-Boat captains had first reported that they were being attacked as soon as they started to transmit their sighting reports. Then they had been disbelieved because the scientists did not think that a high-frequency direction-finding set could be installed in a ship. But this time the lack of liaison between the *Kriegsmarine* and its scientists proved fatal, and U-Boat losses rose alarmingly.

Shipping Losses and U-Boat Sinkings July 1942–June 1943

Month	No. of Ships	Tonnage	U-Boats Sunk
1942			
July	96	476,000	11
August	108	544,000	10
September	98	485,400	11
October	94	619,000	16
November	119	729,100	13
December	60	330,800	5
1943			
January	37	203,100	6
February	63	359,300	19
March	108	627,300	15
April	56	327,900	16
May	50	264,800	41
June	20	95,700	17

Defeat was conceded when the U-Boats were ordered to withdraw for 'regrouping'. There was no disguising the fact that the U-Boat Arm had been shattered by the pounding it had received, and it was necessary to restore morale with new weapons and tactics before committing the U-Boats again. There was also the problem of U-Boat construction to consider, and Hitler and Admiral Dönitz met in a series of conferences to

(52 ships) and the fast HX-229 (25 ships). Both convoys were heading eastward, and on 16 March they were about 120 miles apart. HX-229 was the first to be attacked, and in a space of eight hours 12 ships were torpedoed, *U-338* managing to sink four ships with only five torpedoes. In a desperate attempt to fight off the ceaseless attacks the escorts ordered the two convoys to combine, but even so 140,000 tons of shipping was sunk, and only one U-Boat was sunk by the escorts. A similar attempt was made against the next Halifax convoy, HX-230, but the weather was so bad that it lost only one straggler, while an American escort carrier helped SC-123 to pass through a gap in the U-Boats' patrol line by using her high-frequency direction-finding gear to locate the U-Boat which was transmitting the sighting reports.

The support groups which had been withdrawn for Operation Torch were now being thrown back into the Battle of the Atlantic. By the end of March there were five support groups and three escort carriers in the Western Approaches. They were just in time, for Admiral Dönitz had almost achieved his great dream of shattering the convoy system. After the disastrous battle around HX-229 and SC-122 the Admiralty nearly abandoned the convoy organisation, for it seemed that the U-Boats had found the answer. Half a million tons of shipping was sunk in the first 20 days of March, far more than the Allied shipyards could make good if losses had continued at that level. Just as the U-Boats sensed that victory was within their grasp it eluded them, and they were overtaken by a stunning defeat.

The reasons behind this dramatic reversal were complex. In an attempt to cope with the growing weight of air attack the U-Boat Command had introduced a radar search-receiver, the Metox, which could detect some radar pulses and so warn a U-Boat before the aircraft came into range. So much confidence was placed in the Metox that some U-Boats were even fitted as 'flak-traps' with a heavy antiaircraft armament. Although the ruse was successful against the first unwary Sunderlands and Liberators which came in too close it was not long before aircraft took to circling just outside gun range, while calling up the nearest support group. If the U-Boat tried to break off the action by diving the aircraft immediately switched to the attack.

In March a U-Boat reported that she had been attacked at night by a Wellington bomber, and that the Metox receiver had not recorded any radar emissions. It was this action which prompted the order to stay on the surface and fight it out with enemy aircraft, but a month later came a whole series of night attacks which were undetected by the Metox. In response to urgent requests the scientists replied that there was no possibility of an Allied breakthrough in radar. A chance remark by

DIE WEHRMACHT

HERAUSGEGEBEN VOM OBERKOMMANDO DER WEHRMACHT

Die Schläge der deutschen U-Bootwaffe hat jetzt auch die nordamerikanische Schiffahrt zu spüren bekommen

decide on naval policy. In April 1943 it was established that by the second half of the year production of Type VII boats would be increased to 27 per month, and that this rate could be maintained even if the more complex VIIC$_{42}$ design was built. By 1945 it was hoped to increase production to 30 boats per month, but Dönitz reminded the Führer that the program was using 4500 tons of steel per month for the hulls, and a further 1500 tons for torpedo-bodies.

In June the vexed problem of manpower was discussed, and Dönitz pointed out that even if 40 U-Boats could be delivered each month this would merely exacerbate the shortage of personnel. The current allocation was 102,984 men, whereas the requirements would be for 437,822 men, a shortfall of nearly 335,000. If 634 U-Boats were to be manned 62,000 men would be needed for their crews alone. The Admiral pointed out that since April 1942 the *Wehrmacht* had received the major share of manpower, leaving the *Kriegsmarine* short of 200,000 men. The officer-candidates who had entered the navy in the fall of 1939 were now being given commands, and it would be necessary to transfer officers from the other two services. If the personnel were not found the U-Boat Arm could function but at the cost of manning none of the new surface craft such as motor torpedo boats completed after January 1944.

In July 1943 Dönitz made the first mention to Hitler of a startling new project, the so-called electro-submarine. Known as the Type XXI, it was a fully streamlined boat with a novel 'figure 8' hull and enlarged battery-capacity to give it a much higher underwater speed. Another important feature of the design was the provision of automatic torpedo-reloading gear, which enabled a Type XXI boat to fire torpedoes rapidly at a series of targets, unlike the older boats which had to retire to reload, with each torpedo taking half-an-hour to load. This feature alone made the new submarine a lethal weapon against convoys, and Hitler demanded that the *Konstruktionsamt* should try to improve on the November 1944 delivery date for the first. Albert Speer was told to authorize three-shift working in the shipyards in order to get production up to 20 per month, and it was hoped that these new U-Boats would eventually win back the initiative from the Allies.

Another advanced design was in hand, the Walter turbine design known as the Type XVII. The Walter turbine burned enriched hydrogen peroxide and oil fuel with a catalyst to release sufficient oxygen, thus providing a 'closed cycle' to dispense with the need for outside oxygen. This provided a very high underwater speed, 20 knots or more, because of the great heat produced during the decomposition of the hydrogen peroxide. The fuel was known as *T-Stoff* (abbreviation for *Trieb-Stoff*), Ingolin or Aurol, and proved both difficult and expensive to manufacture. An experimental boat, *V-80*, ran trials in 1940, and *U.791* (ex-*V.300*) was the first U-Boat to be fitted with a Walter turbine for trials in 1942. The first production model was the Type XVIIB coastal boat displacing 312 tons, which needed 55 tons of Aurol to reach 21½ knots for 150 miles.

The Walter turbine boats must, however, be judged an aberration, despite their advanced technology. The German Navy was already badly behind in its submarine building-programs, despite all the efforts made in the shipyards, and the Walter boats rank with some of Hitler's tank projects as pipe-dreams which frittered away resources and delayed production of more useful equipment. There is no doubt that 50 Type XXI U-Boats in mid-1944 would have done more to redeem the situation than 200 Walter boats in 1945. To compound the error the shipyards were allowed to continue the construction of the now-obsolescent Type VIIC, and 'diluted' or mixed skilled and semi-skilled labor was used to build the highly complex Type XXI boats. Heavy Allied bombing on shipyards also held up

Left: The incomplete hulls of Type XXI U-Boats lie amid the devastated shipyards of Hamburg after the city's surrender in May 1945.

production, and as a result only four Type XXI boats had been completed when Germany surrendered in May 1945. The first, *U.2511*, did not finish her training and shakedown until the week before the surrender. A simplified version with a single hull, known as the Type XXIII was also built, and the small numbers of boats completed proved quite successful in British coastal waters but so few were available that they could not affect the outcome of the war.

The only other countermeasures that could be initiated in 1943 were the provision of new weapons and tactics. New acoustic torpedoes were introduced to allow U-Boats to attack escorts, but technical problems made them less dangerous than first thought.

In the search for an answer to the danger from aircraft someone remembered the Dutch *schnorkel* device which had been installed in submarines which had been captured in 1940. The device was by no means perfect, and had to be modified by the Germans because the air induction pipe and the exhaust 10 feet below the surface created a clearly visible wake. This problem was successfully tackled, and the *schnorkel* device was soon made a standard fitting for U-Boats.

The *schnorkel* achieved its aim, but it made life extremely uncomfortable for U-Boat crews. In rough weather the valve shut constantly, and each time the diesels sucked in enough air

Right: The schnorchel head of *U.516*, a Type IXC.
Below: Two Type XXIII boats, *U.2336* and a sister, lying at Lisahally, Northern Ireland, in 1946.

Above right: A blazing merchantman settling by the stern is viewed from the attacking U-Boat.
Above, far right and right: Following a mid-ocean rendezvous between two U-Boats, a life raft ferries mail to one of the boats.

to create a partial vacuum which made ears and eyes pop. It also had the effect of making the U-Boats 'keep their heads down' for longer periods, so that although they became harder to sink, in turn they sank fewer ships. But the U-Boats never gave up, and they remained dangerous right to the end. More than 32,000 officers and men out of a total of 39,000 died on active service. The balance sheet was a grim one:

U-Boats built:	1162
U-Boats sunk:	784
Allied Warships sunk:	175*
Merchantmen sunk:	2828*
Merchantmen sunk:	14,687,231* tons

*These figures include sinkings by Italian and Japanese submarines, but they form only a small part of the total.

No figures exist for the total number of merchant seamen lost, because the Allies' merchant fleets included vessels from so many neutral nations, but some idea of the scale of losses can be gauged from the fact that the British Merchant Navy alone lost 30,248 men in action.

On 7 May 1945 Admiral Dönitz, now the Führer as well as Commander in Chief of the German Navy, transmitted orders to all U-Boats to cease hostilities. For the second time in 30 years the U-Boats had failed in their bid to defeat the world's navies and were destined to finish their careers in enemy ports. Some refused to accept the surrender orders and scuttled themselves, while *U.977* went to South America to be interned rather than surrender, but the majority surfaced, hoisted the black distinguishing flag agreed with the Allies, and handed themselves over to the nearest warship to be escorted to port.

THE WAR AGAINST JAPAN

When the Japanese attacked the US Pacific Fleet at Pearl Harbor without warning on the morning of 7 December 1941, it was envisioned that submarines would play their part in supporting the aircraft carrier strike. The Submarine Force was to move to the vicinity of Hawaii in order to provide reconnaissance for the Carrier Striking Force and to attack any US warships which presented themselves. One unit was detailed to launch midget submarines against Pearl Harbor itself, but as we shall see the attack was unsuccessful and all were sunk.

At the outbreak of war the Japanese submarine fleet numbered about 75 operational units. A large construction program was in hand, with 18 boats to be ready by the end of 1942 and a further 11 to be ready by the end of 1943. What was lacking was any real grasp of the importance of standardizing and streamlining production, such as the German, British and American Navies had already achieved in their submarine programs. The Japanese High Command seemed to be unduly obsessed with the potential of their big boats, but whatever designs were chosen the shipyards were not able to build fast enough. The *RO.35* Class was intended to be a standard medium design, and the first was laid down in October 1941 and completed in March 1943, but 8 out of the 18 ordered were not completed until 1944. A large number of additional boats authorized in 1941 were cancelled in 1943, never having been laid down. By comparison a typical American *Gato* Class boat, the *Barb* was laid down in June 1941 and completed a year later, and the British were taking 18 months to complete a 'T' boat.

The American Navy had gone to the opposite extreme. Having developed their fleet submarines through a series of logical improvements to the 'T' and 'G' Classes of 1940–41, they were content to put the 'G' Class into quantity production as the *Gato* Class. Then when war-experience dictated improvements the new *Balao* Class and their successors the *Tench* Class were kept as similar as possible. Although only four builders undertook the construction of the *Gatos* they proved well able to meet the challenge. Two other yards had to take some of the burden

when orders were placed for a total of 366 *Balao* and *Tench* Classes but this does nothing to diminish the remarkable American achievement of 228 submarines completed in four and one-half years.

Unlike the Japanese the Americans had no chance to use their submarines in conjunction with the battle fleet. After Pearl Harbor there was no American battle fleet in the Pacific, and the submarines were the only units which could fight back. For a while the attack was blunted because of a high incidence of failures affecting the Mark 14 torpedo. In some cases the

gyroscopes failed, and in others the warhead pistol failed to function, and until these problems were identified and cured the submarine offensive was only partially effective. But once an improved torpedo was available American submarines began to make enormous inroads into Japanese shipping.

Although American submarines did not hesitate to attack warships they were given instructions to concentrate on mercantile shipping, particularly oil tankers. The Japanese had carved a seaborne empire for themselves, and their large merchant fleet was needed to supply the garrisons in all the outlying islands. Furthermore, Japan imported 20 percent of its food, 24 percent of its coal, 88 percent of its iron ore and 90 percent of its oil. The Japanese Navy had not foreseen that this fragile structure could be so vulnerable to a concerted submarine attack, and had failed to devote any resources to antisubmarine warfare. As a result US submarines were not subjected to the full weight of countermeasures that were the lot of a U-Boat in the Atlantic or a British submarine in the Mediterranean. At the end of the war the Americans were amazed to learn that the Japanese claimed to have sunk 486 submarines. The actual losses were 37 sunk by enemy action and 23 through miscellaneous causes such as grounding.

In 1943 American submarines first used wolf-pack tactics against Japanese shipping. Because of the lack of convoying and the poor antisubmarine measures used by Japanese escorts there was no need for the large packs used by the Germans in the Atlantic, and the Americans found that groups of three were suitable. Under such titles as 'Ben's Busters,' 'Donk's Devils,' 'Ed's Eradicators' and 'Laughlin's Loopers' the packs ranged far and wide across the Pacific in search of targets. Their names

Right: The launch of a new submarine for the US Navy. US shipyards built over 200 boats in 1942–45.
Below: The *Sea Devil* (SS.400) rescues aircrew from a rubber dinghy in the Pacific.
Bottom: The USS *Cavalla*, a *Gato* Class fleet submarine runs on the surface.

derived from the aces who led them, and several boats like *Barb*, *Rasher*, *Silversides* and *Tang* sank over 90,000 tons of shipping. The highest scoring US submarine was USS *Tang* (SS.306), with 100,231 tons, and by 1945 the Japanese had lost over 4,000,000 tons of shipping.

American submarines were able to attack on the surface at night, just as the U-Boats had in 1940, but unlike the British escorts the Japanese did not get radar sets until very late. Using their own radar the US submarines could choose their position for attacking, and dodged the escorts with ease. Some daring commanders were expert in the 'down-the-throat' shot, which involved firing a full salvo of six torpedoes at an attacking escort at close range.

As the Japanese came to rely more and more on small junks and coasters for shipping cargoes the big American boats found themselves short of targets. But by early 1944 the British and Dutch had established three flotillas in the Far East. Although smaller and shorter on range, the British and Dutch boats proved capable of operating within the 10-fathom line. Their most notable successes were the sinking of the cruisers *Kuma* and *Ashigara*, but they also achieved the destruction of a large number of minor vessels.

The American submarines, in addition to their onslaught on merchant shipping, performed a vital role in reporting enemy fleet movements. Time and again fleet commanders received vital intelligence from submarines, and it was these patrolling submarines which scored some of the greatest successes of the Pacific War. In 1944, just on the eve of the Battle of Leyte Gulf the *Darter* and *Drum* ambushed a Japanese heavy cruiser squadron, sinking the *Atago* and *Maya* and damaging the *Takao*. In June 1944 the *Albacore* torpedoed the new carrier *Taiho* during the Battle of the Philippine Sea, causing severe damage which led to her loss, and five months later the incomplete *Shinano*, a 62,000-ton converted battleship, was torpedoed by the *Archerfish* in Japanese home waters.

The Japanese submarine force, from which so much had been expected, had little to show by comparison. By concentrating on attacking well-defended formations of warships they exposed themselves to the efficient antisubmarine tactics of the Americans, while their neglect of mercantile targets reduced the burden of escort. American antisubmarine measures were very much better than the Japanese, as demonstrated when a newly commissioned destroyer escort, the USS *England* sank six submarines in 12 days in 1944. On 19 May the *England* sank *I.16*, 140 miles northeast of Choiseul Island in the Solomons, and acting on the likelihood that the submarine was one unit in a patrol line she moved west. On 22 May she made another sonar contact 250 miles north of Kavieng in New Ireland, which turned out to be *RO.106*. A day later she sank *RO.104* in the same area, followed by *RO.116* the day after that, 25 miles south. At about midnight on May 26, north of Manus Island she caught *RO.108*, but for her last kill she moved back to the scene of her earlier successes, and sank *RO.105*, 200 miles north of Kavieng.

Against this, credit must be given for some outstanding Japanese successes, particularly the sinking of the damaged carrier *Yorktown* by *I.168* during the Battle of Midway and *I.19*'s destruction of the carrier *Wasp* south of the Solomons in 1942. The battleship *North Carolina* was damaged by a hit from *I.26* and one of the greatest successes came right at the end of the war, when on 30 July 1945, the heavy cruiser USS *Indianapolis* was sunk by *I.58*. The Americans had become so used to

Top: The USS *Ray* (SS.271) under refit at Mare Island, with alterations ringed in white.
Above right: Submarines built at Manitowoc, Wisconsin, were launched sideways into the narrow river.
Above: The *Argonaut* (SS.475) in April 1945.
Below: The famous USS *Barb* (SS.220) leaves Mare Island, California, on her last war patrol, July 1945.

enjoying immunity from submarine attack that they had allowed this valuable warship to travel without escort between Guam and Leyte, and even failed to notice that she was missing for three days.

As things got worse for the Japanese they turned to desperate measures. Submarines were sacrificed in useless attacks on invasion fleets or used to run supplies of goods and ammunition to garrisons of small islands. Although this misuse of submarines was justified in the case of Malta in 1941–42 the Japanese had so many garrisons that they were forced to use more and more of their submarines for this subsidiary purpose. A special supply-submarine was developed the *I.361* Class, which could

steam 15,000 miles on the surface and carry 82 tons of cargo. Nor did the dispersion of resources end there; the army started to build its own submarines for supplying its garrisons. By 1945 most of the fleet submarines were converted either to supply craft or transports for *Kaiten* midgets.

When World War II ended in August 1945 it also brought to a close the most successful submarine campaign in history. Only 231 Japanese merchant ships survived out of a prewar total of 2337 ships listed in *Lloyd's Register*. In all 190 submarines were completed for the Japanese Navy by August 1945, but only 55 were surrendered, a loss rate of more than 70 percent. It was a heavy price to pay for so little.

THE MIDGETS

The Italian Navy was the first in the field with midget submarines in 1912, with two 18-feet boats designed for the defense of Venice. During World War I the Italians built a further 12 midgets for harbor defense, but nothing further was heard of midgets until the mid-1930s, when the Japanese started work on two at Kure Dockyard. The result was the Series A, numbered *Ha.3* to *Ha.44*, 78-feet, battery-driven craft armed with two 18-inch torpedoes. They were designed to be carried by seaplane tenders and fleet submarines, and were intended for the penetration of enemy harbors. Their first operation was a disaster, an attack on Pearl Harbor intended to coincide with the main air strike. No midget got into the harbor and four were sunk. An attempt to attack Sydney Harbor, Australia, in May 1942 was also unsuccessful, although a torpedo intended for the US cruiser *Chicago* did sink a ferryboat. An attack 24 hours earlier on Diego Suarez in Madagascar had greater success; two midgets from the submarines *I.16* and *I.20* hit the British battleship *Ramillies* and a tanker.

More midgets were built, but mainly for local defense, in which role they achieved little. In 1944 the growing realization that the Empire of the Rising Sun was coming ever closer to defeat led to the construction of a new series, the Type D or *Koryu*. A total of 540 were planned but by August 1945 only 115 had been finished. As a counterpart to the *Kamikaze* tactics of the Air Force the Imperial Navy produced the *Kaiten* series, basically the body of a Type 93 24-inch torpedo adapted for one-man control. The prototype could travel 26,000 yards at 30 knots, or as much as 85,000 yards at 12 knots, and had a massive 1½ ton warhead. Later models used a hydrogen peroxide motor in place of the gasoline and oxygen motor, giving a maximum speed of 40 knots, but the shortage of engines meant that many *Kaitens* ended up as fuel tanks. The *Kairyu* midgets were more like the original Type A and carried torpedoes slung underneath the hull. Over 200 were built at Yokosuka Dockyard but like the other types, they did little to stave off defeat.

The Italians also revived the midget submarine just before World War II, and even entertained an ambitious project to ship one on board a submarine to attack the US east coast harbors. But their most noteworthy achievement was the *Maiale* or 'pig,' a small midget submarine which had two saddle-positions for its crew. Although known as a 'human torpedo' (*Siluro a Lenta Corsa* = Slow-running Torpedo) the 'pig' bore no resemblance to the Japanese *Kaiten*; it merely looked like a torpedo, and the 'warhead' had to be detached by the operators and clamped to an enemy ship's hull. In December 1941 three 'pigs' from the submarine *Scire* succeeded in penetrating Alexandria Harbor, and disabled the British battleships *Queen Elizabeth* and *Valiant*. In fact the battleships were sunk, and the Italian Navy had eliminated the entire British battle fleet in the Mediterranean, but because they were resting upright on the bottom of the harbor Italian Naval Intelligence erroneously assumed that they had only suffered minor damage, and so a great victory was therefore thrown away. The other success scored by Italian 'pigs' was against shipping in Gibraltar. In an elaborate undercover operation the Italian crews operated from the tanker *Olterra* in neutral Algeciras harbor. Two freighters were sunk and one damaged by this attack in early August 1943.

Ironically the skill of the Italians was put to best use against their own ships. After Italy negotiated an armistice with the Allies in September 1943 several Italian warships fell into German hands, and Italian crews were used to sink the cruisers *Gorizia* and *Bolzano* at La Spezia in June 1944.

The British had shown no interest in midget submarines until the Alexandria attack in 1941, which led to a series of special underwater assault craft. Two were ideas which had already been put forward, a one-man midget, and a four-man midget, the third was a straight copy of the Italian pig, code-named the Chariot. The one-man midget was known as the Welman Craft, and was designed to attach its 560 pound charge to the target by magnetic clamps. The Chariot was transported in a cylinder welded to the casing of a submarine, as in the Italian submarines.

The large midgets were known as X-Craft, and they differed from all other navies' midgets in not using torpedoes. Instead they were fitted with two 2-ton side charges which were faired into the saddle tanks. Once under the targets the X-Craft could release the charges internally and merely drop them on the floor of the harbor; with charges of such a weight there was no need for them to be exploded in contact with the hull to inflict serious damage. A slightly enlarged version known as the XE-Series

Above right: This *Seehund* midget submarine is preserved at Washington Navy Yard.
Right: Two surrendered *Seehunden* on road trailers enabling them to be rapidly deployed.
Far right: A section of a Type XXVIIB *Seehund* midget submarine.
Below: This Japanese Kaiten midget is preserved at Washington Navy Yard.

54

was built later for Pacific operations, with air-conditioning to improve habitability.

Chariots were used in October 1942 in a daring attempt to cripple the German battleship *Tirpitz*, which was hiding in a fjord north of Trondheim. A Norwegian trawler managed to tow two Chariots past the German outposts, but a sudden squall made them unmanageable, and they had to be abandoned. In September 1943 six X-Craft were sent to attack the *Tirpitz* and the *Scharnhorst* in Kaafjord. One, *X-8* had to be scuttled on the way to Norway and *X-9* dived and was never seen again, but *X-5*, *X-6*, *X-7* and *X-10* left their towing submarines to begin the 50-mile voyage through minefields and nets. Unfortunately *X-10* had to abandon the attack when she was only six miles from the battleship's anchorage, leaving three to make the final attack. *X-5* came to grief about a mile from the *Tirpitz* but *X-6* and *X-7* laid their charges underneath her giant hull before being scuttled by their crews; both were damaged and had no chance of escaping back down the fjord. When the charges went off they inflicted heavy damage on the *Tirpitz*, and although she was patched up she never put to sea as a battleworthy unit again.

In November four Welman craft attacked shipping in Bergen without success. These little midgets were unreliable, and never achieved any results; like the Chariots their operators suffered from the extremely cold temperatures experienced in northern waters, whereas the X-Craft, although uncomfortable, afforded reasonable protection to their crews. In April 1944 the submarine *Sceptre* towed *X-24* to Bergen, where the midget attacked a floating dock and a transport. The transport was sunk and so *Sceptre* and *X-24* returned for a second time in September; this time the floating dock did not escape.

Chariots were successfully employed in the Mediterranean. In January 1943 five penetrated Palermo harbor in Sicily, sinking the liner *Viminale* and the incomplete light cruiser *Ulpio Traiano* at their moorings. Only prompt action by their crews in removing limpet mines saved the destroyer *Grecale*, the torpedo boat *Ciclone* and the submarine *Gemma* from damage. In the Far East the *Trenchant*'s Chariots sank a transport at Phuket, in Thailand, and *XE-1* and *XE-3* attacked the heavy cruiser *Takao* in Singapore in July 1945.
Olterra in neutral Algeciras harbor.
K-Craft (*Kleine Kampfmittel* = Small Assault Units) as a countermeasure against invasion but they never played a decisive role. There were several types. The *Neger* was a one-man torpedo with a torpedo slung underneath, which ran awash with the operator in an open cockpit. About 200 were built, and later models had a perspex dome over the cockpit. The *Marder* was similar but could run submerged. *Negers* claimed two patrol vessels off Anzio and a destroyer off Normandy, while *Marders* sank the Polish cruiser *Dragon*, four landing craft and four minesweepers off the Normandy beaches. About 300 *Biber* one-man midgets were built, 29 feet craft armed with two under-slung torpedoes. They could be carried on deck by U-Boats and are credited with sinking 95,000 tons of shipping in the Scheldt estuary between December 1944 and April 1945.

The most successful German midgets were the Type XXVIIB *Seehund* type, which were developed from the XXVIIA or *Hecht* type. They were 39 feet craft propelled by a single-shaft diesel-electric plant, and when extra fuel tanks were fitted had an operational radius of 500 miles at 7 knots.

A swivelling rudder made them extremely maneuverable, and it was found that depth-charge attacks tended to throw them violently aside without sinking them – an experience which must have been extremely unpleasant nonetheless for the two-man crew. *Seehunds* sank the French destroyer *La Combattante* and a British LST in the Thames Estuary in February 1945. Nearly 300 were completed and several served in the Soviet and French navies after World War II.

Left: The nuclear submarine HMS *Repulse* has a Deep Submergence Rescue Vehicle (DSRV) perched on the after casing.

Above: A British XE-Craft is pictured running in Sydney Harbor in 1945.
Right: A Japanese Type A midget lies stranded on a Pacific island beach, 1943–44.
Bottom: The depot ship *Titania* with the X-Craft carrying submarine *L.23* lying alongside.

THE NUCLEAR AGE

As soon as German resistance ceased in May 1945 teams of American, British and Soviet submarine experts converged on German dockyards and shipyards. They had only one aim, to locate and recover as much information as they could on the new Walter boats. The British and Americans each raised a sunken Type XVIIB boat, and the Soviets certainly recovered at least one.

Everybody knew how far the Germans had progressed with their revolutionary designs, and it was solely a question of who got there first. In the end the British and Americans got the lion's share as they occupied the principal yards and harbors well to the west of the advancing Soviet armies. A share of the British tonnage was, however, later handed over to the Soviets in 1946.

It was the Walter hydrogen peroxide engine which interested everybody, despite the problems associated with it. Both the British and Americans succeeded in making their captured boats work, and the British even built two improved versions subsequently, but the Russians are believed to have abandoned their efforts after a lengthy period of trials. Looking back now it can be seen as a waste of time and money for the unstable nature of the fuel combined with its bulk made the submarine the dangerous and short-legged weapon that it had been before the introduction of diesel engines. Nevertheless it was the only means at the time of producing the high speed needed to counter the ascendancy of antisubmarine tactics.

Below: A Soviet 'Foxtrot' Class diesel-electric powered submarine edges through the Arctic pack-ice in 1973.

The basis of the Walter system was the chemical hydrogen peroxide, a relatively unstable compound which breaks down easily into water and oxygen, the breakdown being accompanied by the generation of considerable heat. In normal industrial use a 35 percent solution could be produced, but any greater concentration needs stabilizers which form protective layers around any contaminating particles such as dust or rust. High Test Peroxide (HTP) was the name given to the very high concentrations of hydrogen peroxide needed by the Walter turbine. The fuel was a colorless liquid considerably more viscous than water, and liable to explode if its temperature rose above 200° Fahrenheit. To make matters worse a fire could not be put out by smothering it with foam or even sand, as the oxygen generated in the reaction was sufficient to maintain combustion, and the only way to deal with it was to dilute the HTP with water and so stabilize it.

Despite all the problems the British pressed on with their two HTP-fuelled boats, the *Explorer* and *Excalibur*, built in 1952–58, but they spent their time as 27-knot underwater targets, acting as stopgaps until the first British nuclear submarine could give antisubmarine forces similar target-speeds.

The influence of the Type XXI design was ultimately far more important than that of the Walter boats. The Type XXI characteristics were incorporated in new construction as fast as possible. The Soviets designed their *Whiskey* Class and its later variant the *Zulu* type to incorporate virtually every feature. Other navies, notably the Americans, adapted the design as far as possible to fit in with their own ideas. In 1946 the US Navy began its 'Guppy' program, named from the acronym for Greater Underwater Propulsive Power; as an alternative to building

Above: 'Whiskey' on the rocks: this Soviet submarine grounded off Karlskrona, Sweden, in December 1981.
Right: A Soviet 'Charlie' Class nuclear cruise missile submarine in the South China Sea, 1974.

large numbers of new submarines nearly 50 of the 200 wartime submarines of the *Gato*, *Balao* and *Tench* Classes were rebuilt to incorporate Type XXI characteristics.

The basic approach in the 'Guppy' program was to streamline the hull and increase the underwater power. They lost their conning towers and instead were given a streamlined 'sail' which enclosed the periscopes and a schnorkel mast. The characteristic buoyant bow was replaced by a round bow and

Top: 'Foxtrot' submarines number some 60 boats and they are seen world-wide.
Above: The torpedo compartment of a modern British nuclear submarine, showing the reloading gear.

every conceivable piece of equipment likely to cause resistance was either removed or made retractable, down to deck-cleats. Internally it was much harder to find space for a bigger battery as the wartime fleet submarines were by no means spacious.

The success of the prototypes led to a further 22 *Balao* Class boats being converted. There was even a 'Pearl Harbor Guppy' a simple conversion undertaken at the Pacific Fleet base which involved removal of deck guns and platforms and crude streamlining of the periscopes.

The 'Guppy' configuration became standard for submarines throughout the world. The British converted their 'T' and 'A' Class boats similarly, and even when navies could not afford the expense of a full conversion the deck gun was sacrificed and the conning tower became a slender fin. The schnorkel or 'snort' (its British name) also became a standard fitting but with many improvements over the original German version.

Nothing had come of a German project late in the Second World War for U-Boats to tow submersible rafts across the Atlantic to act as launching pads for V-2 rockets, but the US Navy pushed ahead with the idea of firing guided missiles from submarines. In 1947 a submarine fired the first surface-to-surface cruise missile, the Loon. This small missile, an improved version of the German V-1 'doodlebug,' could be carried in a watertight 10 feet by 30 feet canister on deck, much like the old aircraft hangars of the 1920s, and then launched from a collapsible ramp by a rocket booster; it was assembled on deck and then 'flown' by radio signals, either from its parent submarine or another boat to its target. Although a crude weapon in that it could be jammed or even shot down by existing antiaircraft defences, the submarine-launched Loon and the later Regulus I and II were the forerunners of the most lethal submarine weapon of all, the underwater-launched ballistic missile.

Apart from experimental conversions of older *Gato* Class boats to such exotic uses as cargo carriers, underwater oilers and amphibious transports the other major effort the US Navy was making was the most revolutionary idea of all, the use of nuclear propulsion. Work on a reactor capable of harnessing the immense power of nuclear fission at a controllable rate had started in January 1948. Development of the associated tech-

Above: The hull of the first Trident missile submarine, the USS *Ohio*, dwarfs even a 4000 ton *Los Angeles* SSN.
Below: A Soviet 'Foxtrot' is shadowed by an American destroyer in the Mediterranean.

and the *Nautilus* (SSN.571) was launched by Mrs Eisenhower on 21 January 1954 at Groton, and only eight months after that she was commissioned. She was an immediate success, and in her first year steamed over 62,000 miles. Apart from the streamlining of her hull she was very conventional in her design, with two shafts driven by steam turbines using superheated steam provided by a single nuclear reactor. An electric motor and batteries were provided for emergencies; by a strange quirk of history steam propulsion had finally justified itself in submarines.

From the moment at 1100 hours on 17 January 1955 when she slipped her moorings and signalled to the Submarine Force Commander 'Underway on nuclear power' the *Nautilus* began to set records and to break many long-standing ones. On her shakedown cruise she made the longest submerged cruise at the highest speed, 1381 miles to Puerto Rico at an average speed of 16 knots. By 27 November the same year she had logged 25,000 miles, and Rickover, now a Rear-Admiral, could claim that 'The *Nautilus* is not merely an improved submarine, she is the most potent and deadly submarine afloat. She is, in fact, a new weapon. Her impact on naval tactics and strategy may well approach that of the airplane.' And yet, technically, she was no more than an enlargement of the previous *Tang* Class, with six 21-inch bow torpedo tubes and a big BQS-4 passive sonar in the bow. But the figures speak for themselves: in April 1957 when the uranium core of the reactor was replaced she had logged 62,562 miles, while the second core lasted another 91,234 miles.

Of all the exploits of the *Nautilus* none caught the world's imagination like her voyage to the North Pole. On 23 July 1958 she left Pearl Harbor, passed through the Aleutians and the Bering Sea and surfaced only when she reached the shallow Chukchi Sea. She submerged when she spotted deep water alongside the pack ice and headed north along the 12,000 feet deep Barrow Sea Valley. Two days later Commander Anderson told his crew that *Nautilus* had reached 90 degrees North, the exact site of the North Pole, but that there could be no flags or landing parties for the submarine was underneath a 35 feet thick roof of ice. Film of the adventure gave an impression of a translucent cloud of fantastic shapes, dimly lit by the 24-hour sunlight above. Only on 5 August, two days after reaching the Pole, could Anderson announce to the world '*Nautilus* Ninety North'. She had been submerged under the polar ice for 96 hours and had travelled 1830 miles.

It had been a risky business, and had only succeeded after five attempts between August 1957 and June 1958. There was the obvious risk of collision by surfacing underneath the ice pack but much more serious was the risk of colliding with unknown hazards in the deep Arctic channels. These were totally uncharted waters and the *Nautilus* was travelling virtually blind, with no navigational aids beyond echo-sounders and a TV camera to allow the captain to look up at the ice. If she had been badly holed by a pinnacle of rock or had damaged her propellers far under the icecap there was no other submarine in the world capable of reaching her, and her crew would have shared the fate of a previous generation of polar explorers.

More experimental nuclear submarines followed, to evaluate different types of reactor. A fifth, the giant 5450-ton *Triton* (*SSN.586*), broke all previous records by having two reactors; in 1960 she made an incredible underwater voyage around the world lasting 84 days. She submerged off Long Island on 16 February and proceeded to the St Peter and Paul Rocks in mid-Atlantic where the circumnavigation began on 24 February.

nology was in the hands of a group of scientists and engineers at the Naval Reactors Branch of the Atomic Energy Commission, led by Captain Hyman G Rickover of the US Navy. The penalty for failure would be immense for not only was a large amount of money involved but also the prestige of the United States, but Rickover and his team never showed the slightest hesitation.

On 12 December 1951, when the Navy Department was satisfied that the time had come to order the hull it announced that the name chosen would be *Nautilus*. This commemorated not only two previous US submarines but also the mythical boat of Captain Nemo in *Twenty Thousand Leagues Under the Sea*. Her keel was laid on 14 June 1952 by President Truman at what had now become the Electric Boat Division of General Dynamics, the birthplace of the Hollands. Work progressed rapidly

Left: The new nuclear attack submarine *Jacksonville* (SSN.699) lies alongside the Trident missile submarine USS *Ohio* at the Electric Boat yard, Groton, Connecticut.

The circumnavigation was completed on 25 April and she surfaced on 10 May.

Despite such feats the early nuclear submarines did not have the most efficient hull-forms for underwater speed, largely because they were derived from existing ideas on streamlining. At about the same time as the final designs for the *Nautilus* were being prepared work started on a small submarine designed to test new hydrodynamic principles. She was the *Albacore*, and when she appeared at the end of 1953 her appearance caused a great deal of surprise. She had a whale-backed hull with no deck-casing, and even the streamlined 'sail' had given way to a much thinner dorsal fin. Her two propellers were contra-rotating on a single shaft, and she bore a noticeable resemblance to the original British 'R' Class of 1918, with a hull made up of tapering circular sections, much like a small airship or 'blimp.' In fact many of the ideas tested by the *Albacore* derived from earlier aerodynamic research on dirigible shapes. Since refined into the standard 'tear-drop' form, the new hull-form provides significantly higher speed and maneuverability from the extra power now available.

The Soviet Navy had been very impressed by the massive U-Boat campaign in the Atlantic and spent the years after World War II in building up a large fleet to replace the one which had performed so dismally in the war. The lessons of the German Type XXI and Type XVII boats were absorbed, but the HTP experiments were discontinued after some years of abortive investigations. Like the Americans the Soviets grasped the

Right: The Polaris boat *Van Steuben* (SSBN.632) returns to Charleston Navy Yard, South Carolina, at the end of an extended deployment in 1965.
Below: The 1000-ton Swedish submarine *Näcken* is small enough to be lowered into the water by crane.

The 'tear-drop' hull design became standard, but another problem had to be overcome, that of noise. The first nuclear boats like the *Nautilus* were very noisy, partly because of the turbulence caused by the inevitable holes in the casing and the design of propellers. Propellers 'sing' from the effects of cavitation, and today a computer can scan the recorded 'signatures' of all types of ship to give a quick identification of ship-type and the speed at which it is travelling. Russian submarines have the reputation of being very noisy, the old *Whiskey* type being compared to an express train passing in the distance. Sound travels far underwater, and the *Nautilus*, for example, could be heard ten miles away when using pumps to cool her reactor. Great emphasis is now placed on propeller-design to eliminate cavitation, but the need to let water into ballast tanks means that a submarine must have a number of holes in its outer hull.

However impressive the tally of nuclear submarine building by the two Super-Powers it would be wrong to assume that there is no future for the conventional submersible. Not only are the 'nukes' expensive to build, they also make demands on skilled manpower which all navies are finding hard to meet. The inevitable bulk of the reactor and the steam machinery needed for high speed makes the nuclear submarine very big, yet there are areas like the Baltic, the North Sea and Mediterranean and Black Sea where a 3000-ton submarine is at a severe disadvantage on account of her draught and size. The Russians are rumored to be considering a new conventional class for defense and the smaller navies still rely on them to defend their coasts.

It is hardly surprising that the nation which has made the most original contribution to conventional submarine design is Germany. Although the Federal German Navy was not permitted to build submarines when it was first formed as part of NATO in 1954 this restriction was soon waived to permit 350-ton boats. The Federal German Navy had no need to repeat the effort of the 1920s to conceal its researches, for NATO gave its blessing to a rapid re-forming of a U-Boat Command. Two Type XXIII U-Boats which had been scuttled in the Western Baltic were raised in 1956, and as the *Hai* (Shark) and *Hecht* (Pike) they were recommissioned in 1957 for training. At the same time a Type XXI boat, the former *U.2540* was raised and put back into service as a non-operational trials vessel under the distinguished name *Wilhelm Bauer*.

Above: The British nuclear hunter-killer HMS *Churchill*.
Far left: The SSBN HMS *Repulse* enters Portsmouth.
Left: A circular hull-member for the first Trident SSBN is lowered into place at Groton, Connecticut.
Right: The ultimate sanction, an A.3 Polaris missile.

potential of nuclear power, and in 1958 they completed the first of the *November* Class, 3500-tonners. The *Victor* Class which appeared in 1967–68 were much quieter than the *Novembers* and are believed to be capable of 30 knots underwater.

The only other countries to embark on the construction of nuclear submarines were Great Britain, France and possibly the People's Republic of China. The British and French both have surface fleets of considerable size, and wished to develop the nuclear submarine not only as a defense against Soviet nuclear submarines but also to give their antisubmarine forces proper experience. It is becoming more and more obvious that the hunter-killer submarine is not only the best craft to catch another submarine but also the ideal Sonar platform. During operations in the Arctic in World War II, Allied escorts noticed that U-Boats were often able to hide under 'thermal layers' formed by layers of water of differing temperatures. When water changes temperature it changes density, and this can deflect sonar pulses. Surface ships have to be equipped with variable-depth sonar to avoid this effect, whereas a submarine simply changes depth. She is also relatively unaffected by rough weather as there is virtually no wave effect below periscope depth.